TEENAGE
COMPETITION

TEENAGE COMPETITION
• A Survival Guide •

SUSAN & DANIEL COHEN

M. EVANS AND COMPANY, INC.
New York

Library of Congress Cataloging-in-Publication Data

Cohen, Susan.
  Teenage competition.

  Bibliography: p. 141.
  Summary: Examines the positive and negative aspects of
competition in areas of adolescent life such as
academic success, family life, and social status and
suggests ways of choosing how to compete in a healthy way.
  1. Competition (Psychology) in youth—Juvenile literature.
2. Interpersonal relations—Juvenile literature.
[1. Competition (Psychology) 2. Interpersonal relations.
3. Adolescence] I. Cohen, Daniel. II. Title.
BF724.3 . C63C64   1986   155.5   86-24307

ISBN 0-87131-487-8

M. Evans and Company, Inc.
216 East 49 Street
New York, New York 10017

Design by Diane Gedymin

Manufactured in the United States of America

9 8 7 6 5 4 3 2 1

CONTENTS

1. The Gullery and the Cafeteria   7
2. "Mom Always Liked You Best"   15
3. "My Son the Genius"   26
4. How Do You Measure Up?   40
5. The Chosen Ones   56
6. How You Play the Game   69
7. "And Everything Nice"   86
8. "Be a Man"   100
9. Cliques and Clubs   108
10. Playing Your Own Game   121
11. How to Compete and Survive   134
      Bibliography   141

•1•

THE GULLERY
AND THE
CAFETERIA

To begin the subject of competition among teens, we are
going to start with birds—no bees, just birds.

Have you ever seen a place where herring gulls build
their nests? The gulls generally pick an undisturbed, flat
area, near water, often on an island. Here they gather in
great numbers, hundreds, sometimes thousands of them,
to build nests on the ground. Such spots are called gull-
eries.

Generally you can hear a gullery before you see it, for
herring gulls are extremely noisy creatures. At first sight
the gullery appears to be a scene of chaos. There are gulls
sitting and walking and occasionally flying. Most of them
are squawking or making some other sort of noise, for no
apparent reason. Some gulls stand up straight and raise
their wings slightly; others hunch down and flatten their
feathers. Some gulls stand alone with yards of open space
around them. Others are crammed together in certain
sections of the gullery. It all seems quite random, without
any purpose.

But scientists who have been studying the behavior of
the herring gull have learned that the apparent chaos of

the gullery is anything but disorganized commotion. Most of what the gulls are doing is quite purposeful, and most of the actions involve competition for space, for mates, for food, for attention, and for status. Sometimes gulls fight, but if all the gull's competitive activity involved actual fighting, the gullery would be awash in blood and feathers, and the herring gulls would doubtless have wiped one another out long ago. So the gulls have developed all sorts of signs and signals to take the place of fighting and to let all the gulls know who's who and what's what. Often the human observer doesn't know what's going on. But the gulls seem to understand perfectly.

Those gulls standing all alone are older male gulls that have claimed an area ten or fifteen yards across as their "territory." No other gull enters the territory without "permission" from the older gull. That group of gulls all clumped together—they are a "club" of young unmated gulls. If one of the young gulls enters the territory of an older gull, the older gull stands up tall and points his beak downward. This is a "threat" posture. This usually causes the younger gull to crouch and stretch his neck out in an "anxiety" posture. This is generally followed by a rapid retreat.

These are just the simplest and most easily observable actions. The gullery is a complex web of competition, of action and reaction.

Why have we started a book about competition in your world with a description of the actions of a bunch of birds? There are two reasons: First, to indicate that competition is an important part of the lives of *all* social animals—gulls, wolves, reindeer, chimpanzees, and even human beings. Competition is biologically based. It's in our genes, just as it is in the genes of the gulls. Second, we wanted to illustrate how competition can go on almost constantly; yet an untrained observer, an outsider, may not have the foggiest notion of what is really happening. Among human beings some competition is obvious—in sports, for example, or in arguments and fights. Most competition in daily life is much more subtle, but it's still there.

Let's imagine an intelligent observer from some distant planet, one who knows just about as much about human behavior as you know about the behavior of herring gulls. Now let's put this imaginary observer into the cafeteria of your high school at noon. What would he see? What would he hear? What would he think?

He would probably think that he was observing a scene of noisy chaos—for like the gullery he would probably hear the cafeteria before he could see it. There would be a mass of kids doing all sorts of different things. Some would be crammed around tables, eating and chattering with one another. Others might sit alone in silence. Still others would be walking about, waving and nodding at one another or staring or looking away.

Even the most patient observer of herring gulls has a lot of trouble telling one gull from another, though the gulls seem to have little trouble with this. Our imaginary observer from another world, once he got over the notion that all human beings look alike, probably would find it fairly easy to spot individuals in your cafeteria. There are differences in size, color, and clothing, though sometimes there would be groups where the clothing is so similar that the observer might have real difficulty telling one individual from another. Still, it would take our extraterrestrial watcher days and perhaps months of patient observation before even beginning to figure out what was really going on. The cafeteria, like the gullery, is a complex web of competition, of action and reaction. Most of it is quite subtle. Fights, even open arguments, are comparatively rare in most school cafeterias, but that does not mean that there isn't a constant struggle going on.

If our extraterrestrial observer were astute enough, he would eventually begin to notice some patterns in behavior. Some of those tables would appear to be more desirable and popular places to sit than others. People were sitting at the popular tables because they wanted to, not because they were forced to. There would rarely be an empty place at these tables, and people from other parts of the cafeteria would often be stopping by to talk or wave. Those who ate alone or in small groups rarely got visitors.

When the observer was able to figure out what different human expressions and gestures meant, he would be able to see that those at the popular tables looked more assured, even cocky. The loners would often be downcast and, in extreme cases, frightened. In the cafeteria, unlike in the gullery, being surrounded by a crowd is generally a symbol of high status.

With patience the observer might be able to pick out the meaning of all sorts of signs. When two boys meet in a narrow corridor between tables, does one back off, even if the movement is ever so slight? Are there individuals who seem to take the long way around, just to avoid passing certain tables? Verbal clues could also tell the observer much, but he would have to understand tone and context as well as the words themselves. When one girl says to another, "Oh, how nice!" she can mean just what she says. But with a different tone, the words can mean, "So what" or "How did you get so lucky, you creep."

A FACT OF LIFE

Whether we like it or not, competition is quite simply a fact of life—others' lives—and your life. As far as we can determine, competition has been a driving force in every society at every period in history. In some societies, competition is minimized and sometimes the existence of competition is even denied, though it is there nonetheless. At other times and in other societies, competition is extolled as the great force for progress. We live in a society in which competition is held in very high regard. At this particular time in our history exceptional stress is being laid on the values and virtues of competition. You are supposed to compete—and win!

Is this good or bad? Are we too competitive or not competitive enough? This sort of question has been debated endlessly. We have no simple answers to give you, and we suspect no simple or universal answers exist. While some competition is biologically based, the degree of competition in which we engage is under the control of our society and ourselves.

We do know that competition, or our attitude toward it, can be extremely confusing. You are urged to "go for it," become a winner, excel. Yet often the very same voices that are telling you to go out and win also tell you to obey the law, play by the rules, and be fair.

Sometimes we wonder how stupid do adults really think teenagers are. All you have to do is look around you to see all sorts of successful people—winners—business people, politicians, athletes—who have won by bending or actually breaking the law, ignoring the rules, and not being fair at all. Most of us actually admire the clever and successful cheat, so long as he or she doesn't go too far and, of course, doesn't get caught. In a world where winning often seems to be everything, comparatively little attention is given to how you win or what you win. We are going to try to pay some attention to that subject.

The emotions unleashed by a highly competitive situation are not easy to turn off. Obvious examples are the fights that break out in the stands during and after a

11

football game. Players and fans alike are all fired up for a game. A football game, or any other sport, is a competitive event to be carried out in a limited space and time, under strict rules. But sometimes we actually come to hate the players on the other team and their fans.

In school we compete with others for grades, positions, social status. Sometimes the competition is "clean," that is, free of personal animosity. Usually it's not. Competition breeds jealousy, pride, anger, greed—a virtual catalog of negative emotions. It can make you act in ways that are sneaky, spiteful, underhanded, and just plain nasty. Sometimes it's the same at home. You compete with your brothers and sisters, even your parents, for attention, affection, money, space, whatever. The competition is not always friendly.

On one hand, you are told to compete fiercely; on the other, to be a loving individual. That's not always easy; sometimes it's not even possible. You can't turn competitive drives on and off like a faucet.

Most of you have probably been brought up to believe that you should be good and kind, that goodness and kindness will be rewarded, and that you don't have to be a S.O.B. to succeed. That's what might be called the "official" view of the world. Unofficially, however, you have undoubtedly heard that it's a "dog eat dog" world out there and that in order to compete successfully you really do have to be mean, nasty, and rotten. There is a whole group and style of books telling people how to intimidate, trick, or in some other underhanded way get an upper hand with the competition, be it a business competitor or a spouse. It struck us that books of this type are a form of nonsexual pornography. They are written "for adults only" and, of course, are read and believed by huge numbers of adults. But as a teenager you aren't supposed to know about the ugly side of competition—yet. Of course you do—but the double standards and contradictory messages can be extremely confusing. We'll try to sort matters out.

In preparing this book, we ploughed through (and we are afraid that's the best way to describe it) an enormous number of self-help books about competing successfully, being a winner, being a success, and so forth. You might get the impression that there are a huge number of different kinds of "success techniques." But when you get past the differences in style, practically all these books tell you pretty much the same thing: All you really need to win is to think like a winner—develop a positive mental attitude. This subject is approached with almost religious fervor. The authors of these books say that talent, intelligence, background, and education are all secondary; what really separates the winners from the losers is *attitude*. One "winning attitude" author writes enthusiastically, "Talent is cheap. . . . The world is full of talented alcoholics. . . . Education . . . is for sale . . . the world is full of educated derelects." Sure there are talented alcoholics, but there are even more untalented ones. There are doubtless some well-educated derelects—but the vast majority have little education. This idea—that all you really have to do is spring out of bed in the morning and say "Today I'm going to become a winner" and you will become one—is nonsense. And sometimes it can be harmful nonsense.

Of course, being cheerful, optimistic, and confident will help you compete successfully in practically any field, but talent, intelligence, background, education, hard work, and oh yes, luck, help a lot too. The mental attitude promoters make you feel that if you're not a big success it's because you don't have a "winning attitude." Naturally it's hard to maintain a "winning attitude" if you keep getting kicked in the teeth. There are things about life that simply cannot be wished away.

If there are winners in competition, there are also—inevitably—losers. Chances are you're going to come up losing more often than you're going to win, and handling that is a big part of life. You've got to know how to lose without being a loser.

While competition is an inescapable part of everyone's life, some of us thrive on it. Others shrink from it. If you're a shy, noncompetitive person, there are no simple techniques, no quickie attitude changes that are going to turn you into Mr. or Miss Assertion. While all competition cannot and should not be avoided, you have to be extra careful about picking those areas in which you chose to compete. Don't feel guilty if you can't play all the games.

In this book we are going to look honestly and candidly at the subject of competition and how it affects your life. For make no mistake about it, from sports to sex, you live in a highly competitive world.

We can't offer you any psychological gimmicks that are suddenly going to make you a "winner"—we don't believe that such gimmicks do any good. If there really were a formula that could make anyone a winner easily, there would be no need for the hundreds of different formulas that have been touted by self-help promoters.

What we are going to do is look at a wide variety of competitive situations—the kind that come up in your life—and examine the best ways of handling them. There will be no exhorting, no moralizing.

We are also going to help you take a look at yourself in competition—not whether you win or lose—but how you react to competition.

While competition is unavoidable and is probably a good thing, you can make choices about where and how you wish to compete. What we would like to do is help you make the right choices.

• 2 •

"MOM ALWAYS LIKED YOU BEST"

Can you imagine a real-life family without competition? Parents wouldn't push their kids to play on the football team, earn good grades, or win popularity contests. Brothers and sisters would never disagree. Husbands would defer to their wives. Wives would never envy their husbands. No mother would ever flirt with her daughter's boyfriend. Grandparents wouldn't prefer grandchild A to grandchild B. Sibling A who was flunking every course in school would be only too delighted that sibling B had a 96 average. Sibling B wouldn't mind in the least that sibling A went to three proms in a row while sibling B had to stay home and watch TV reruns of old sitcoms about happy families. Nobody in the family would ever quarrel over who got to make the next phone call or who had been talking too long. Parents and kids would float around being nice to each other and boring each other to death.

Fortunately, there is no family completely free of competitive pressures. Up to a point competition is a necessary and positive component of family life, teaching people how to get along with others, goading them into action, pushing them toward greater independence, making them smarter, stronger, and tougher. Parents in low-income jobs often scrimp and save for years so their children can have

15

the chance to get an education and succeed, thus competing through their children. Unless the pressures on the
kids are too severe, this is a very healthy form of competition and so is much of what psychologists have labeled
sibling rivalry.

RIVALRY—GOOD AND BAD

Ann was a top student. She set the tone for her younger
sister, Peggy. Though Peggy resented getting the old "Are
you going to do as well as Ann?" routine from her teachers, she had a lot of pride, so she worked hard to prove she
was as bright as her sister. As a result Peggy finished
second in her class. If it hadn't been for the competitive
struggle between the two sisters, Peggy would have been
content to settle somewhere around the middle of the
class. That would have been a waste because she had the
ability to be at the top.

Unlike most teenagers, Courtney, seventeen, was in no
hurry to learn to drive. She enjoyed being chauffeured
around by her parents and boyfriends. But her younger
brother was more than ready to learn, and the day he
turned sixteen he applied for his driver's permit. Courtney
couldn't bear the idea of her little brother gaining any
advantage over her, so she got her learner's permit, too,
and enrolled in the driver's ed course at school. Now she's
looking forward to getting her licence and will soon be
fighting with her brother over who gets to use the car.

Though it may seem to you that family competition is
not as important in your life as it once was, don't under-
estimate it. Okay, you probably do worry more about competing with your peers and friends than competing with
your relatives, but you probably remember just how potent
rivalries within the family used to be when you were a

young child. As a teenager you're separating yourself from your family, growing up, reaching out to a wider world. But family relationships are so basic and so intense that they can set the tone for the way you will relate to people the rest of your life. Right now the old tug-of-war between you and your parents and between you and your sisters and brothers may be affecting you more than you realize.

Take sibling rivalry. It's ancient history that began on day one. Do you remember the first time you saw your kid brother or sister? From the moment he or she gurgled up at you from the crib, which had once been your very own possession, you probably felt that the kid was a little creep destined to cause you great anguish and misery forever. Granted, the most rivalrous of young siblings often feel stabs of affection for each other and the battles sometimes cool down by adolescence, with major brawls becoming minor disputes. It's even possible for brothers and sisters to become quite fond of each other when they grow up. But the old wounds don't heal completely, and in some families the competition between kids can have serious and long-lasting repercussions.

Vance

Evan and Vance were two years apart in age. From the start Evan was quiet and obedient, while Vance was active and rebellious. By age six, Evan was considered "the good boy" in the family, whereas four-year-old Vance was labeled "bad." Not that their parents put things in quite such blunt terms, but that's how they behaved. Evan got the praise and Vance got the swats.

The boys remained opposite types right into high school. Evan got good marks. Vance bombed out of most of his courses. Evan was on the student council. Vance was a jock. Everything Evan did seemed right as far as his parents were concerned. Everything Vance did was wrong. Evan's room was neat. Vance's was a mess. Evan didn't go out with girls much. He stayed home studying. Vance stayed out late, picking up girls and getting drunk. It's hardly surprising that Vance grew to resent his brother or that Evan wished Vance would go away. In the end that's precisely what happened. Vance left home.

Sick of being the family scapegoat, he moved in with an aunt and uncle when he was in his senior year of high school. Not only did the move free Vance from living in Evan's shadow at home, he no longer attended the same school. So he was able to establish his own identity and find what worked for him.

Interestingly, Vance's uncle and aunt had no use for Evan. They considered him a nerd. So what if he was a good student; they far preferred Vance's athletic skills. As for personality, they liked Vance's outgoing fun-loving style, his way with girls. They thought Vance's parents were crazy for preferring Evan to him.

The kid on the outs in one family might be the family favorite somewhere else. Families are often unfair. Since you have no control over which kind of family you're born into, you may find yourself in the same spot as Vance, through no fault of your own a loser in a competitive struggle with a brother or sister. If so, there are ways you can make things better for yourself, even if you can't move out of the house the way Vance did. You're old enough now to spend a lot more time away from your family. You can get a job, become active in extracurricular school activities, seek out adults outside your family to confide in, and make new friends who will like you and appreciate you the way you are.

Competing with brothers and sisters is one thing, competing with parents another. Parents who view their kids as rivals set up a whole range of conflicts. Some fathers can't even play a friendly game of softball with their children without turning the game into a do-or-die competitive challenge where winners triumph and losers are humiliated. Mothers can compete destructively with their children, too.

June

June was vivacious and pretty, and at fifteen she had plenty of boyfriends. Her mother, who was still attractive, relived the days of her youth through June, but not as an observer. She kept getting involved in June's relationships, gossiping about boys, asking prying questions, hanging around when they came over to see her daughter. When June went out with a particularly good-looking boy, her mother would invite him to dinner. After dinner she'd join June and the boy on the couch and watch television, meanwhile making jokes, showing off her sexy figure, and generally making it very confusing for the boy. Was he out with June or her mother?

Luckily June's mother never let things go further than a light flirtation and June solved the problem by refusing to discuss her dates with her mother and by making sure she and any boy in her life avoided dinners and evenings at her home.

THE NEW FAMILY

In the past two decades structural changes in the patterns of family life have caused the problems spawned by competition to become more complex than ever before. For starters, most kids today have mothers who work outside the home. That means brothers and sisters have to handle their feuds on their own without adult intervention. Sometimes kids can cope well on their own, but when they can't, sibling rivalry can be scary or even dangerous.

Lenore

Lenore, fourteen and a freshman in high school, was five feet two and weighed one hundred pounds. Her brother, Darren, thirteen and in eighth grade, was five feet eight and weighed one hundred and fifty pounds. Though some boys act older than their age, Darren didn't. He was sulky and sometimes violent.

Darren was going through a particularly tough time, and whenever Lenore came home from school, she found him sullenly reading comic books. When she tried to hold a conversation with him, he snapped rude insults at her. Their arguments had a tendency to turn violent, and Darren would haul off and slug his sister hard. Considering his size in comparison with hers, this was no joke, and the battles usually sent Lenore to the telephone in hysterics to complain to her mother. Lenore's parents did their best to protect Lenore and still keep the channels of communication open to Darren, but there's no getting around it: the fights would have been easier to stop if an adult were home when they happened.

In the old days of the extended family, Lenore would probably have had a grandmother or aunt living in the house who would be there to keep an eye on things when both parents went out to work. In the modern world the best solution for Lenore would be a community center because it would give her a place to go to get away from her brother after school. But places that provide supervision and recreation for young teens are in short supply, and the best arrangement Lenore was able to work out for herself was going to her best friend's house after school as often as possible.

Vince

A high divorce rate has added a new dimension to competition within the family. When parents remarry, teenagers are apt to inherit a lot of new relatives fast. It isn't easy to sort them out. Sixteen-year-old Vince and his brother lived with their mother and stepfather. They got along reasonably well except when Vince's stepfather's daughter from his previous marriage came to visit. Not that Vince minded Sara, who was fifteen and very attractive. Quite the opposite. He wanted to go out with her. Under the circumstances this would have been difficult. Though Vince and Sara weren't really related to each other, they were expected to see each other as brother and sister, not as boyfriend and girlfriend.

Vince's mother posed another problem. She resented Sara terribly, and whenever Sara came to stay with the family, Vince's mother became very competitive. Clearly she considered her second husband's daughter a rival. Between Vince's attraction to Sara, Sara's attraction to Vince, and Vince's mother's attitude toward Sara, family strains were acute. The upshot of the whole mess was that Vince's mother finally lost her temper and swooped Vince and his brother off to stay at a motel whenever Sara came to spend a few days with her father. This enraged Vince, puzzled his younger brother, upset Sara, and gave Vince's stepfather a colossal headache. Throw in one irate mother of Sara and her second husband and Vince's real father, who responded to the complaints of Vince's brother, and you get the American family version of politics in Beirut.

21

Ashley

Or take Ashley who at fifteen was an only child whose parents were divorced. Ashley's father was a charming alcoholic who flitted in and out of her life. Since Ashley lived with her mother, it was her mother who got stuck with all the responsibilities. Sad to say, she never let a day pass without reminding Ashley of this and letting her know just what she thought of her ex-husband. Ashley much preferred her father, maybe because he wasn't around all the time.

Then a bomb went off in Ashley's life. Her father married a young woman barely out of her teens, and a few months after the wedding the woman gave birth to a baby girl, Ashley's little sister. Fifteen is old for a bout of sibling rivalry when you never expected to have a sister or brother at all, and Ashley was hurt and jealous. She was also jealous of her father's new wife. Not only was Ashley afraid of losing the small amounts of attention her father allotted to her, but she had to listen to her mother's daily announcement that maybe at last Ashley could see which of her parents really loved her.

Brad

If you think Ashley had problems, consider Brad. When he was sixteen, he discovered he had a brother his own age he'd never heard of. It seems that before Brad's father married his mother, he had lived with a woman who became pregnant. One day she turned up on Brad's doorstep with Brad's half brother in tow and introduced herself. Brad found it all an exciting adventure, and at first his parents behaved generously. Soon Brad and his brother, Carl, were buddies. Unfortunately, even with the best of intentions, relationships can turn sour.

As the months went by, Brad's mother accused Brad's father of being taken in by Carl's mother. Was he really sure Carl was his son? Carl became jealous of Brad because Brad lived in a two-parent household and seemed to have everything Carl wanted. Through all this, Brad was patient. He really liked Carl. Then came the day when the money Brad's father had saved to buy Brad a car went to Carl's mother because she had lost her job. Brad began to feel the smoldering symptoms of sibling rivalry. The smoldering turned to raging fire when Brad's father started taking Carl to baseball games alone.

If any of these situations reach you where you live, remember you're not alone. A large percentage of your generation is going through the same things you're going through and asking the same questions. There are no easy answers because nobody, including the experts, really knows how to handle these new kinds of family relationships. But be consoled. The family unit has changed drastically before and still survived. We'll all learn to adapt to the different kinds of relationships emerging these days. It won't be easy, but we're a highly adaptable species.

Besides, before long you'll be able to make your own decisions about how to treat the relatives in your family network. That's one of the advantages of growing up. It will be your choice which parent, stepparent, sibling, half sibling, aunt, uncle, blood relative, clan member, or just plain friend means the most to you. You'll be close to some of your kith and kin. Others you'll stay in touch with. Some you won't see at all. But, come on, lots of intact families where divorce is yet unknown have their share of stresses and strains and relatives who've grown apart.

PUSH AND PULL

If some families are hotbeds of competitive pressures, other families withdraw from competing. For every family that pushes a kid to succeed, there's another one pulling a kid back. Arthur's family lived in a tight-knit ethnic neighborhood in a big industrial city. He wasn't encouraged to get high marks. What was the point? He was going to work in the family deli, no ifs, ands, or buts.

Any sign of competitive spirit or ambition in any member of the family was nipped in the bud. Arthur's older sister dreamed of becoming a doctor. The family allowed her to become a nurse. When Arthur picked up a girl at a movie theater who wasn't from the old neighborhood, his parents were upset. He was encouraged to go out with a girl who lived on the block and who went to his school and church. Staying with your own kind, Arthur was told, was safe. Venturing afar was dangerous.

Arthur liked to draw, but his parents refused to let him take art lessons because he'd have to go across town to the museum to study. There he'd meet a lot of weird people who, Arthur's parents were convinced, took drugs and did unnameable things. Arthur's parents had never met an art student, but that didn't stop them from jumping to conclusions.

Considering how much Arthur's family warned him about the terrors of the world outside their neighborhood, it's a wonder he was ever able to leave his house. But Arthur was basically ambitious and quite able to handle competition. He had no intention of hiding away from life. So he joined the navy. It was his way of making the transition to a life that offered wider options. Once out, he'd go on to college and study technical drawing.

Russ's family was very different from Arthur's. Russ's

parents were successful lawyers, highly competitive people, and very sophisticated. They had so much drive that
they weren't satisfied until they had the best house in their
suburb, threw the most lavish parties, drove the biggest
cars, and made and spent the most money.

Russ was the beneficiary of his parents' success. From
the time he was born, he had it all. You name the toy and it
was his. Computers, video equipment, cameras, stereos,
and cars followed. He took art lessons, piano lessons, went
to fancy camps, toured Europe with his parents, played all
kinds of sports, and was whisked off to a tutor with a Ph.D.
the minute he fell behind in math. College? The sky was
the limit. His parents could afford the very best. Russ's
brother got the same royal treatment. He, too, was pressed
to excel.

With all these advantages, was Russ a great success? He
didn't measure up in his parents' eyes, but with such standards how could he? Unlike his parents, he knew when to
stop. Russ studied hard but not obsessively, ending up
thirtieth in his class of 280. Considering that he went to an
outstanding and very competitive top high school, that was
a respectable showing. Anyway, it satisfied Russ, who was
smart but no brain. Russ got into a good but not a great
college, yet he liked it. His parents wanted him to go into
medicine, but Russ wasn't sure what he wanted to do. He
took his time finding out. To escape from competitive
pressure, he went horseback riding or shot videos, hobbies
he enjoyed for their own sake. He finished with an attitude
to competition a lot like Arthur's. If Arthur had to learn to
put himself forward, Russ had to learn to hold himself
back. Arthur found out that there are contests in life, and
Russ figured out how to keep life itself from becoming a
contest. Both were winners despite their families.

•3•
"MY SON THE GENIUS"

"**D**o your homework?"

Sound familiar? No doubt you've been hearing these words from as far back as the day in elementary school when you received your first homework assignment. Parents have been known to whisper this famous phrase, announce it, shout it, bellow it, or accompany it with bribes of chocolate chip cookies and larger allowances. There are exceptions. Some fathers have been known to worry more about their son's ability to play football than about the grades he gets. There are still mothers around with the old-fashioned idea that daughters should be pretty air-heads out to hook a guy. But, by and large, parents really care about academics so much so that even easygoing otherwise tolerant parents (who don't mind if their kids keep pythons as pets or go around bald with their skulls tinted purple) panic over low grades.

ACADEMIC COMPETITION

On the surface, academic competition looks clear and straightforward. Concentrate, study a lot, work hard, and you'll do well. But as you know, it's far from that simple. In some schools a top student is admired by his or her teachers and peers. In some schools top students are ignored, bullied, and labeled nerd of the year. Sometimes the pressure to succeed academically is so great that teens crack under the strain. To make the picture even more confused, bright kids are not always top students and top students are not always particularly bright.

Some kids get good marks because they pick up information easily and have good memories. Others get good marks because they know how to charm and manipulate adults, including at least some of their teachers. Teachers after all are human. Like other people you'll meet throughout life—including bosses, co-workers, and friends—teachers aren't textbook pure. There are good ones, bad ones, and those in-between. While we're at it, we want to make clear that getting an education and getting high grades are not necessarily synonymous. When most parents talk about doing well in school, they usually mean getting good grades. But you could define a good student as someone with a deep interest in a particular subject, a person who analyzes ideas and subjects them to criticism. Alas, in this imperfect world the person who duly memorizes the subject matter, never contradicts his or her teacher in class, and turns in a neat, methodical, but inherently mediocre paper may get an "A"; whereas the student with an original point of view who argues with his or her teacher and who can't be neat to save his or her life may very well get a "B" or lower on an assignment. You've probably seen this happen or perhaps even been the person getting the "B" or lower.

Then there's the added problem of trends and fashions. What is a good education, anyway? Sometimes the war cry is back to basics and strict standards. Sometimes the call is to free the imagination and encourage the creative spirit. This can be very confusing. There are even fashions in career choices. These days a lot of kids are told to study something practical and go into business, medicine, or the law. You can't help but be influenced by this pressure. It's all around you. American kids are now told to emulate the Japanese who work very hard in high school preparing for tests. Not that tests are an unknown to American students.

Actually things are far from rosy in Japan where academic pressure has been blamed for a rising suicide rate and severe psychological problems. As to the idea of being practical, well it is true that American teenagers today face a tighter job market and less student aid than in the recent past. But you are not an object that can be shaped and twisted to meet the latest fashion. If your talents lie in music, acting, painting, writing, or the study of history rather than in science, computers, or accounting, then why should you choose a career in science, computers, or accounting? You must find what's right for you. People who are pushed to go into fields that are wrong for them or who are pushed to get marks that are unrealistically high can wind up hating what they do and losing confidence in themselves.

Stewart

At fifteen, Stewart was one of the top students in his school. He went to a public school in a run-down neighborhood where many students weren't even dreaming of college. There was relatively little academic competition and Stewart thrived. His teachers singled him out for attention. He got high marks, particularly in science courses. Stewart was reasonably but not overwhelmingly diligent. He did his homework, but he still had plenty of time to be with his friends or go watch a ball game. Then came trouble.

Stewart's parents decided he needed a better education than he could possibly get at the local high school, so Stewart's mother got a full-time job and Stewart's father, besides his regular job, moonlighted just so they could send Stewart to a private school. Stewart wasn't sure he wanted to go, but with his parents and teachers telling him what a wonderful opportunity it would be he gave in and enrolled in a private school across the city.

He was unhappy from day one. Though Stewart had been able to shine in his old school, now he was in a tough, competitive atmosphere. When it came to grades, everybody around him showed killer instinct. Instead of firing Stewart up to compete, the school had the opposite effect. He felt hopelessly outclassed and very stupid. Not surprisingly he found it hard to study. Stewart's parents urged him to give the situation time rather than rushing back to his old school. So he stayed and, yes, eventually things got better. But Stewart never fully recovered from the shock of the experience, and he graduated from that private school with lackluster marks and a deep-seated fear of trying to compete in college.

Too bad nobody thought to take Stewart's opinions into account before he was shoved into a competitive situation he was unprepared for. He could have remained in his old school, taken accelerated courses, and aimed for early graduation. Then he would have started college at seventeen. That's one way to get a head start. Another option for Stewart was a summer school program on a college campus. This would have provided him with a chance to test his ability to compete in a tougher milieu. Had things gone well, he might then have considered a private high school.

Justin

Stewart's parents were willing to make great sacrifices for him, possibly too great, and they had an exaggerated view of his ability. But some parents go way beyond Stewart's in misreading their children. Justin was bright, but to his mother he was a genius. She continually bragged about how Justin had read by the age of four and how a famous psychologist had declared Justin a musical prodigy when he was six. Her expectations for Justin were so out of line with reality that by the time he was sixteen he didn't walk, he ran from competition.

Left to himself Justin would probably have done quite well. Though his mother would never have believed it, he probably would have been a solid "B plus" student in a good public school. He would have been popular, too, because he was outgoing, and charming and was considered good-looking. But he went to a highly intellectual private school. Unlike the private school Stewart attended, marks weren't stressed. Individuals were allowed great autonomy. But though the school wasn't rigid, it was intense and Justin felt as if he were being observed under a microscope, with the observers waiting for him to sprout into a mental giant.

Justin withdrew into grandiose fantasies about all the wonderful things he could achieve if he wanted to. Though his piano teacher complimented him on his talents, Justin practiced less and less with each passing day. His poor performance in school was noticed by his teachers. Justin's mother was called into school to discuss his lack of progress. She had a dozen excuses to explain why Justin wasn't working up to potential. It was either the fault of his teachers or he was bored or he was too sensitive to compete. It didn't seem to occur to her that the real reason Justin withdrew from competition was that the standards she had set for him and which he accepted for himself were unrealistically high. Justin didn't dare try because no matter what he did it wouldn't be enough. It was safer just to show promise.

Justin quit school in his junior year; that caused a major family crisis. Justin and his mother had a big fight. A lot of angry things were said with much pain on both sides, but in the end the fight did more good than harm, clearing the air and allowing Justin to take a big step toward maturity. Justin realized he was afraid to work hard because he was afraid of failure. Burdened as he was, what was the point of continuing on an obviously self-defeating path? Better to travel for a year or two and then see what he wanted to do. There was plenty of money in his family, so this was a realistic option.

Justin celebrated his eighteenth birthday in Italy. As he moved around, eventually traveling to India, he took whatever work he could find, met as many people as he could, and had a lot of exciting experiences. He began to assess his talents. Free of his mother's influence, Justin could see that though he wasn't extraordinary he wasn't ordinary either. His self-confidence was still below par, but he was learning to accept himself as he was. In the course of his travels, he had become an accomplished cook. He decided to come back to America and become a chef. Justin wrote his mother and asked her to find out about cooking schools. At first she was disappointed, but eventually she accepted the idea. Besides, she was quite sure that if Justin "the genius" became a chef in no time at all he would write a best-selling cookbook. Justin returned home, got his high school diploma through a correspondence course, and now works in a chic restaurant.

Not everyone's afraid of competition. Some people rel-

31

ish it and get straight "A's." Whether this is good or bad depends on the circumstances. If you have a genuine interest in at least one subject so you're not only going for grades, then it's great. On the other hand, if you're ready to jump off a bridge when you don't get an "A," then you'd better reevaluate your goals. If grades are so important to you that cheating has become a habit, then you may be the academic equivalent of the jock who must win at all costs or the gambler who'll take any risk. We'll spare you a sermon about the moral issues of honesty versus cheating and just remind you that cheating is a wobbly prop to lean on because occasionally schools really do crack down on cheating. If you happen to be the person they crack down on, ouch!

Try to take advantage of the opportunities high school offers you to pursue different interests. We know it isn't easy to do this because many classes are boring. Besides the girl or boy across from you is probably a lot more fun to look at than the teacher and therefore a distinct distraction no matter what the class is like. But you owe it to yourself to find some reasons for going to school other than your parents' telling you to and the law requiring it up to a certain age. Hobbies help. If the only way you can cope with the tedium of school is by reading science fiction, then read away. Who knows, maybe someday you'll not only read it, you'll write it. If French frightens you, but you find fossils fascinating, collect them. Don't let anyone tell you you're wasting your time. Maybe you'll become a paleontologist. We are not suggesting you neglect your regular classwork, but we don't want you to waste four important years of self-discovery because you find the official side of school a bore. Though someday you'll have to make serious life and career decisions, we believe adolescents need time to grow up first. So use the time to find out what's easy for you, what's hard for you, and what you'd like to learn more about.

We know that lots of things besides boredom can get in the way of learning. If you're a black kid in a poorly funded inner city school, or a Hispanic kid for whom English is a second language, you're not going to have the same chance of getting a good education as a white upper-middle-class kid going to a fancy suburban public school or a rich kid headed for Exeter or some other classy prep school. Some students have physical problems, like dyslexia, which make it hard to learn. A lot of stereotyping goes on in schools, even so-called good ones, with some teenagers slotted into the top grooves and other teens routed to a lower track.

Danielle

Danielle loved to write. She poured her hopes and dreams into poems and short stories, filling whole notebooks with her ideas. In a middle-class suburb somebody would have spotted Danielle's talents and encouraged her. Her parents would probably have bought her a typewriter, a computer and printer, and volumes of poetry.

But Danielle wasn't middle-class. She lived in a mountainous rural area where social distinctions are sharply maintained. A few families own most of the local businesses, go to church every Sunday, hold the local political offices, and get elected to the school board. At the bottom end of the social scale are families like Danielle's, where nobody owns much of anything and for generations not a single person has gone to college. In Danielle's family you are lucky to graduate from high school.

Danielle was written off from the very beginning as one of "them" and lumped with the low achievers. Had she been brilliant, it might have been different; but though she learned to read quickly, she was no whiz kid. She wasn't much of a math student. She wasn't glib or outspoken in class. By high school she was mired in "B"-level courses and blocked from taking accelerated English classes because the powers that be agreed she wasn't going anywhere in life and wouldn't need them.

There wasn't much Danielle could do to fight back. The affluent popular clique would have nothing to do with her. Her parents weren't much help. All they expected of her was that she get a job in the diner or at the laundromat, be married by eighteen, and have a baby by the time she was nineteen. Danielle hadn't the foggiest idea of how to work the system on her own. So when she was told she wasn't college material, she believed it. She just happened to love to write and went on creating poems and stories.

It was the new librarian at the public library who first noticed something distinctive about Danielle. The librarian was a newcomer to the community, having recently married the editor of the local newspaper. She was impressed with Danielle's eagerness to read, and she saw to it that Danielle was given a part-time job answering the telephone at the newspaper. Danielle showed her some of her stories, and the librarian encouraged her to send them off to magazines to try to get them published.

As with most of life, nothing magic happened to Danielle. She wasn't discovered by a major publisher. She didn't wake up one morning to find that she was a bestselling author. Her stories remained unsold. But Danielle's attempts to get her stories published helped her gain confidence, and she began to take herself seriously. As a result she became much more assertive at school both with her peers and her teachers. She wrote a page of poetry for the yearbook. She made up her mind to stay in high school the

34

full four years and go on working at the newspaper. A community college in the next county offered evening courses in communications. Meanwhile, she was planning to write a novel. Her world was expanding.

Like Danielle, most people don't have it made. For them there's no such thing as just breezing through school. If you're in deep trouble academically, remember that circumstances change. Later may be very different from now. You can recoup even after a very hard time.

Louise

Louise was extremely intelligent, but her family was a mess and she couldn't concentrate. Her father was an alcoholic who could never hold a job long and who beat her mother regularly. Once Louise watched him push her mother down and smash her head against the concrete pavement. Louise rushed to protect her mother, but when she got in the way she was the one to be hit. After such a grisly existence, is it any surprise that Louise ran away from home when she was fifteen?

Lost in a big city, Louise moved in with a man who sold drugs. She spent her sixteenth birthday bailing him out of jail. When he walked out on her, she finally called the only member of her family she had ever been able to rely on at all, a cousin a few years older than herself. Louise's cousin told her that her mother had finally left her father. So Louise got in touch with her mother, who encouraged her to move in with her. But that was more than Louise could face. Her mother then suggested she move into a halfway house. But Louise had another plan.

If you think this sounds like a perfect recipe for doom, gloom, and failure with Louise winding up an addict or lying dead in a gutter, think again. People can be surprisingly resilient especially when they're young. Louise became an emancipated minor, a turning point in her life. It meant she could stop running. Now that she had special legal rights and responsibilities, Louise got a job as a waitress and moved into an apartment. She went back to school, attending a high school for ex-dropouts where she received counseling. Since her life was now reasonably stable, she was able to learn and learn she did. When she graduates from high school, she's going to a city college. She wants to be a teacher. Of course, she'll have to work long hours to support herself while she goes to college, and that won't be easy. But given her strengths and accomplishments, we're betting Louise makes it.

If someone who has been through what Louise has been through can finish high school and go on to college, others can too. So, if you're doing badly in school for whatever reason, don't despair. Some people think it's the end of the world if they flunk a course or a term. It isn't. You'd probably be surprised at the number of successful people who bombed out in high school. If you can get tutoring and/or therapy now, great. That would be a start. If you must wait to deal with your academic problems until your life is straightened out, okay. That happens. There's more than one way to earn a high school diploma, more than one route to college and a good job.

But what if you're very successful academically? What if you're a top student? Does that mean your life is trouble-free? Of course not. We've already talked about the wear and tear on the overly competitive student who can't be less than best. But even the most relaxed super student is often the target of resentment and jealousy. Bright sensitive teens are often picked on by the school bully, and nobody likes to be called the grind of the class.

Lab Rat and Fat Matt

Lab Rat is thin and nervous. Obviously Lab Rat is a nickname but it stuck. His real name is John. He is first in his class and has been for as long as anyone can remember. Learning comes easily to John. He is also well organized and works very hard, so he deserves to be first. Unfortunately, John's efforts are not appreciated by the rest of the class except when they want to borrow his completed homework or copy off his paper during tests.

John is quiet and gentle. He doesn't like sports and he isn't interested in extracurricular activities. He doesn't go out with girls. He would have, but with a nickname like Lab Rat nobody wants to go out with him. John's best friend is the boy who is second in the class, Matt, otherwise known as Fat Matt. Because they like to look through microscopes, collect rocks, read large difficult books, and use their brains, they are always being teased.

Teachers generally like them, but that only makes matters worse. They are accused of using teacher's pet techniques to grease their way through school. So, despite honors and academic awards John feels lonely, different, and out of step. He doesn't go to parties. No doubt he won't even go to his senior prom. John would probably be better off in the kind of private school where academic achievement is prized. But he wouldn't have an easy time anywhere. He is the sort of kid who is more comfortable with adults than with teenagers. Of course, since teenagers do grow up, John has something to look forward to. He will get older. For people like John, life is often better after high school. In all probability John will succeed brilliantly in college and be free to choose any career he wants. The day will come when he'll find friends. He may even become popular with girls. A straight "A" average can seem rather sexy in college and graduate school. So if you are the Lab Rat or Fat Matt of your class, have hope. The jocks may wish they could trade places with you in a few years.

Lynn

So far we've discussed the *problems* inherent in academic competition, but some students thrive on it and grow. Lynn loved pressure and deadlines. A smart kid with good study habits and lots of drive, she enjoyed competition. It spurred her on to greater heights. She escaped from competitive pressures through jogging, swimming, and going to movies. But when it came time for work, she worked.

Lynn came from a poor family with seven kids, and she was eager to qualify for a scholarship to college. Competition didn't throw her. In class she asked a lot of questions, picking her teacher's brains. She knew that if she ran away from competition she'd never realize her potential. Instead of hating the other competitive teens in her class, she respected them. Even when things grew fierce and there were clashes and quarrels, she kept cool, depersonalizing the situation as much as possible.

It wasn't easy. Other kids accused her of being a grind and a show-off. They laughed at her when she went over "A" papers to see if she qualified for a few extra points. Every time she handed in an extra-credit assignment the burnouts in the class would make obscene jokes. By junior year she was number one in her class, which won the respect of the other academically competitive teenagers in the school. Still, she had to put up with snide remarks from two boys who had been in the running for the top spot. They keenly resented a girl beating them out.

Lynn's biggest scare came when a student from India

transferred into her school. He was as competitive as she was and had terrific marks. Though she liked to think of herself as above petty maneuvers, she sneaked down to the office one morning and checked out his transcript. She was relieved to find out she had a slight edge in grades.

Lynn was lucky that learning came easily to her and that she had the gift to retain what she learned. But she earned her place as valedictorian. No one handed it to her. She had self-discipline, was well organized, and was able to focus. She was always on the lookout for challenges. Take chemistry, a tough subject. Lynn didn't just read text-books. She went to the library and read further, searching for ways to make chemistry come alive and ignite her imagination.

The payoff came at graduation when honors showered down on her and so did money, including a full-tuition scholarship to a good college. It's nice to know that sometimes when you reach for the stars you get them.

•4•
HOW DO YOU MEASURE UP?

Does any of this scene sound familiar to you?

You open the test booklet and glance quickly over the first few questions. You are suddenly hit by a wave of nausea. The words and figures shimmer and grow misty before your eyes. You know that you are in the wrong room, or in the wrong country. All the questions seem written in a strange foreign language. Nothing looks familiar. All those hours spent studying. All that money spent on tutoring. All the self-tests and retests. It's all for nothing. Your mind is a complete blank!

You have just started your SAT—Scholastic Aptitude Test.

The feeling is only momentary. The panic subsides. You begin to recognize some of the questions and become dimly aware of some of the answers. You are beginning to relax, and start marking your answers with your trusty number two pencil. Then you look around you and panic all over again.

Half the kids in the place look as if they're already on the second or third page while you're still on page one. Look at Bobby the Brain over there—he's marking answers at a fantastic clip. You can practically see his eyes glow every time he spots the right answer, and he's laugh-

40

ing to himself! At this rate he'll finish ahead of schedule and even have time to *check* his answers. You're going to be lucky if you answer half of the questions.

You try to force your attention back to the task at hand and block out all the distractions. What's that noise? Somebody's humming and tapping his feet. You look over at the next aisle; it's Doug the Burnout. Why the hell is he even taking this test? He's not going to college anyway. If he does, it will be to some two-year college where they let you in if you can tie your shoes. He doesn't care, he's just guessing and marking his answers at random. He looks relaxed, and that's important. Maybe he'll get lucky and get a good score—better than yours. Things like that happen. If he would just keep quiet, maybe you could concentrate.

What's that girl across the room doing? My God! She's working out problems on a watch calculator. You're not supposed to do that—that's cheating! Where's the proctor? Is she even in the room? There she is at her desk; she looks like she's asleep. Should I tell her someone's cheating? No, that'll waste my time. Besides everybody hates a stoolie. I'd be murdered as soon as I stepped out into the street.

Isn't that guy looking at a dictionary? And how about those two kids going to the bathroom? Bathroom hell, I'll bet they've got a stolen answer sheet hidden out there. I've heard stories about that sort of thing.

Who's that guy taking the test? I've never seen him before. He look's like he's thirty years old. He can't be a high school student. He's older than the teachers. I'll bet he's a ringer. He was probably hired to take the test for someone else. Nobody checked identification. Einstein could have come in here to take the test, and no one would have checked.

I'll bet everybody in this room is cheating except me.

I'll bet they're all going to get higher scores.

Why did I spend all that time studying and getting tutored? I never heard of half this stuff anyway. Who cares what *mordant* means? My whole high school career is going down the drain. I'll never get into college. I'm going to have to join the army.

The scene we have just described is imaginary and exaggerated. But it is not too imaginary and not too exaggerated.

WHAT DO THEY TEST?

Throughout your elementary, junior high, and high school career you have taken a huge variety of tests. But for most students none seems more important and more ominous than the SATs. Most high school students, their parents, and their guidance counselors believe that SAT scores to a large degree determine which college a student will get into and, even more significantly, what sort of college a student *should* get into.

In a high school mythology the SATs don't so much measure what you have learned, they measure your ability to learn. The tests measure your "aptitude," how "smart" you are, your "mental capacity," or simply your "brains." If you have a high test score but low grades in your classes, then you are an "underachiever." If you have low test scores but high grades, you are an "overachiever." The real measure of ability is not what you have actually achieved, but those test scores. They are the *real* you.

If you're a senior and have already taken the SATs, then you know how you use it to compare yourself with others. The Student Report itself, which is mailed to your home, not only gives you your individual score but tells you how you measure up against all the other students in the country. You only got 400 on your math score? Your student report lets you know that miserable total puts you way down in the lower 30 percent of all the students in the country who are planning to go to college. It even puts you in the lower half of all the high school students including those who never passed a math course, have no intention of going to college, and just sucked on their pencil during the test.

On a more personal level, as soon as those reports are mailed home you begin comparing your scores with the scores of everybody you know. There are always a few kids who "don't want to talk about it." You figure they did so poorly that they're ashamed of their scores—and you're probably right.

Then there's someone who has a combined score of 1400 or above. Even if you don't know the person, you can be sure you'll hear about the score. It gets on the school grapevine and everybody knows. If you missed it at school, your mother will tell you. She heard it in the supermarket. The reaction is the usual mixture of admiration and hatred. "Oh who cares, she's a grind. She just studies all the time," you say, as if studying was tantamount to cheating. The unspoken implication is, "Well if I studied that hard, I'd do as well or better. I just have more important things to do."

High scores are sometimes posted by the schools and in smaller communities are often reported in the newspapers. At one time, scores were kept secret, even from the students. Not anymore. Every May it's a big game of "What did you get?" "How did you do?"

Even students who did well are urged, by their guidance counselors and/or their parents to take the tests over again, so they can do even better. For some the SATs can practically dominate a whole high school career.

43

THE ENDLESS SATS

Take Billy—he's been taking the SATs since seventh grade. There is no limit to the number of times you can take the test; all you have to do is pay. Billy's parents are both teachers, and education is important to them. Billy has always been a good student, and his parents hope and expect that when he graduates from high school he will go to one of the top colleges, probably one of the Ivies. Certainly he is expected to go to something well above the rather ordinary state schools his parents attended. Yale is mentioned around the house a lot. No one in Billy's family ever went to Yale, but his father visited it once and thought the campus was "nifty."

Though Billy may wind up at the top of his class, his parents know that the high school he attends is only average, and even being the top of an average high school won't get you into Yale or any of the other highly selective colleges. So they have pinned their hopes and his on the SATs.

He has been in training for them with the same intensity that an athlete trains for the Olympics. He takes the test every time it is offered, and in-between times he studies the various SAT guides and does a lot of self-tests with samples provided by the guides. He plans to take the SAT preparatory course offered by his high school and get special coaching that is offered at a center in a nearby town.

Even if you aren't like Billy, the SATs can eat up a lot of your time and energy. If you're planning to go to college, you'll almost certainly take the test more than once. Then there is the Preliminary Scholastic Aptitude Test (PSAT), a mini version of the SATs. Most kids take the PSATs in their junior year, and many are rated, or rate themselves, on the basis of the PSATs. If they do poorly on the PSATs, they will often scale down their college ambitions. There are also the regular SAT preparatory courses in school, which take time from other classwork, and there are outside courses and coaching, which take not only time, but money and lots of it. Then there are those endless self-tests.

The most popular college guides print the average SAT scores of the entering class of schools covered. These scores may influence which schools you apply to. If the average scores of a particular college are much higher than your scores, you may figure you'll never get into it so you needn't bother to apply. If the college's scores are too low, you may figure it's a school for retards and so reject it. For many prospective students the test scores of a college alone outweigh any other factor in making a choice.

Most high school students would probably regard the SATs as the single most important measure of how "smart" they are. It appears to give an objective scientific ranking of your "brains" and how they compare with the "brains" of others in your school and across the nation.

Everybody seems to take the SATs oh so seriously. Politicians and educators point to "declining test scores" as proof that your generation is going to hell. Then they point to "improving test scores" as evidence that the nation is on the right track.

So the SATs look like they are pretty darned important. Very few who agonize through the three-hour test two or three times, and who groan or glory because of the scores they receive, actually think seriously about what the test really shows—what that score means—what quality of you is being measured.

The name Scholastic Aptitude Test makes it sound as if what is being measured is some innate quality—an aptitude for school work. The old intelligence quotient based upon IQ tests was supposed to measure an innate quality labeled intelligence. But these tests, while they are still in use, have fallen out of favor. They have been shown to be full of biases, and no one could properly define what the quality of intelligence was that the test was supposed to be measuring. Trying to measure innate mental abilities has proved to be a very slippery business.

The SAT isn't exactly a test of knowledge—that is what you've learned during your high school years—either. No test which concentrates on vocabulary and basic mathematical skills could properly be called a test of general knowledge.

The SATs are supposed to be somewhere halfway in between a test of innate ability and knowledge. The official booklet given out to students taking the SATs in New York State says "The Scholastic Aptitude Test (SAT) measures the verbal and mathematical abilities you have developed over many years, both in and out of school." If you think about that definition for a moment, you will realize it's pretty vague. All attempts to come up with a clearer and more precise definition have been unsuccessful. In fact, the Educational Testing Service, which prepares and administers the SAT, has quietly changed over the years its definition of what the SAT is supposed to be testing.

With its precise numerical scores like 560 Verbal and 620 Mathematical the SAT sounds as if it is measuring something real like your height or your temperature or your average bowling score. But the SAT score is nothing like that. The scoring from 200 to 800 is completely arbitrary. The score could be 1 to 100 or 2 to 200.

What makes the SAT seem so impressive is that an enormous number of students take the test and have for a long time. The statisticians and test makers have a mountain of numbers to work with in order to make their tests sound solid and scientific. But they still can't tell you what it is that the tests are really testing. Are they just vocabulary tests and tests of basic calculation? If that is all the SATs are, are they worth all the effort and agony that you pour into them?

Worse yet, the SATs might just be tests of a student's ability to take SAT tests. Some people may not do very well on multiple choice tests because such tests make them nervous or they don't work as quickly. Others may do very well indeed because they are good test takers. But that still may have very little to do with how "smart" anyone is.

HOW ABOUT COACHING?

For a long time the Educational Testing Service claimed that since the SATs tested abilities learned over many years there was no way that the test could be studied for—that is, hitting the books for a solid week before the test wouldn't help. They also said that there was no form of tutoring or coaching that could raise your score and that simply guessing at answers would do you more harm than good. As it turned out, none of this was true.

One of the quickest ways to improve SAT scores is to familiarize yourself with the test—how it looks, how it works, and in general the types of questions that are asked. The better you understand the way the test makers think, the higher the score you will get. For a long time the ETS was very secretive about its tests. It wouldn't allow old tests to be made public. But a law passed in New York State required that the tests be made public. So the ETS has now gone into the business of publishing old tests and tips on how to take the SAT. This is quite a switch for an organization that just a few years earlier claimed that coaching didn't do any good. ETS even prepares a coaching program for elementary school students. Is one of those "abilities developed over the years" the "ability" to take tests?

Recently there has been an interesting development in the field of SAT coaching. A couple of hot-shot coaching services have been developed that claim they can raise a student's score substantially, sometimes as much as 200 points, in just a couple of weeks. As these services freely admit they raise scores by gimmicks, not by increasing the student's knowledge or ability. These services will show you how to answer questions correctly without bothering to read the question. Some might consider it cheating in a sense but it's legal.

One of these services is called Princeton Review. It has nothing to do with Princeton University, though the founder of the service, John Katzman, did graduate from that university. The Educational Testing Service also touts a Princeton connection. ETS officers are located near Princeton, New Jersey, but have no direct connection with the university either.

Katzman says, "Right from the start I tell our kids, 'I'm not a teacher. This isn't school. I'm not going to teach you English. I'm not going to teach you math. I'm going to teach you the SAT.' I tell the kids that they're not competing with each other, they're competing with ETS."

According to Katzman the key to beating the SATs is knowing how the tests are put together. Once you learn that, he says, you can sometimes get the correct answer without even reading the question!

As you can imagine ETS is not happy with people like Katzman. They say that Katzman has used questions that are intended for use on future SAT tests to drill his students. That is illegal and ETS has taken him to court.

Katzman says the attack on him is a "public relations move." The controversy is sure to continue.

But Princeton Review's Katzman is only the most aggressive and outspoken of the SAT coaches. Other services that have been operating for years claim that scores can be raised up to 150 points, after a cram course. ETS rejects such claims.

You might wonder why ETS doesn't just change the test so the gimmicks wouldn't work anymore. But if they did that, then all the statistical consistency the SATs have built up over the years would fall apart. If the 1988 test, for example, was dramatically different from the 1987 test, then how could the scores for the two years be compared? And without years of statistical analysis behind the test, how could the test makers say that the new test was any good? Students could protest with considerable justification that this year's test was harder, or easier, than last year's test. Consistency has been the SATs greatest claim to scientific accuracy. If the test makers have to produce a radically different test every year just to stay ahead of the coaches, the test is in big trouble. The new coaches are confident they can keep ahead of the test makers if they do try to change.

There is even a deeper question. If this sort of gimmick coaching can actually raise scores significantly (and it appears that it can), then is the test really measuring anything worthwhile? Does it really test abilities "developed over many years, both in and out of school"? It certainly does not appear so.

If we don't know what the SAT measures, what does it do—what effect is it supposed to have on your life? Basically, it's supposed to help colleges decide whether to admit you or not. Again according to the official SAT student bulletin:

"These tests are useful because courses and grading standards vary so widely from school to school that making comparisons is difficult. Scores on standardized tests help admissions officers compare the preparation and ability of students from different schools."

Though most college-bound seniors seem to think that their SAT scores will determine which colleges will admit them, the reality is that for the vast majority the scores don't count at all. If you have pretty good grades, some recommendations, some extracurricular activities, and nothing negative, like a long arrest record, you're probably going to get into most schools, because most schools are simply not that selective. Most schools accept the majority of students who apply. If your grades are lousy or you have other problems, an extra 100 or 200 points on your SATs won't help. Indeed, some admissions officers contend that the worst candidate for admission is a student with bad grades but good SAT scores.

Some of the highly selective colleges, those that have more applicants than they can possibly handle, may use the SATs in the process of deciding whom to take and whom to reject. Just how important test scores are is impossible to say, for a college's selection process is usually a quirky one. It's far better to be the son or daughter of a prominent alumnus or alumna than it is to have high SAT scores.

SAT scores are not too bad at predicting how a student will do in his or her first year of college. But your high school grade point average, no matter what sort of school you go to, is probably even a better predictor. So if your performance in high school is the best guide to how well you are going to do in college, then what do you need the SATs for in the first place? It's a good question.

One of the best correlations is between SAT scores and

family income. The more money your family has, the better your SAT scores are likely to be. Does that mean the rich people are smarter than poor people? Those who construct the SAT would certainly deny such an implication. They would quite properly point out that children of well-to-do families tend to go to high schools that are better equipped and better run than the children of poor families. Outside of school the richer kids have many more opportunities to learn than the poorer kids. Simply by having money they tend to have more self-esteem and would be far more relaxed and confident in taking tests. And they can afford fancy coaching, which poor kids usually can't.

The trouble is that the SATs with their aura of being "objective" and "scientific" tend very strongly to reinforce the idea that rich kids *are* smarter than poor kids. No matter what the test designers say, most kids and their parents and their teachers and society at large believe that the tests are measuring something basic and probably hereditary. At the very least people believe the tests measure a student's capacity for hard work. And this belief can be terribly, terribly damaging. It reinforces the idea that people who are poor deserve it because they are stupid and lazy.

As must be obvious, we don't have a very high opinion of the SATs, or other standardized, multiple choice tests. We would love to be able to tell you that such tests can be safely ignored. Perhaps five or ten years from now such advice will be valid. The whole SAT program has been under serious attack from a lot of different sources. The test makers often respond by shifting their position as to what the SATs are good for.

In these days of declining college enrollments and rising costs, many colleges are hungry for students—so for the majority of schools the SATs are less important than they ever were in deciding which students to accept. Some colleges will accept practically anyone who can pay.

A few small but selective colleges have revolted against the tests and dropped them as a requirement for admission. There has been no measurable decline in the quality of the students who have entered these schools. If a couple of the large and well-known colleges also decided to drop the SAT requirement, that might well start a stampede by all sorts of schools to get rid of the test.

The gimmick coaching services present a very real threat. If students who attended the courses regularly score much higher than students who don't, the whole justification of the SATs as a measure of abilities "developed over many years, both in and out of school" crumbles. Those who cannot afford coaching could very reasonably claim that they were being victimized by an unfair system weighted in favor of those who have money.

So these pressures may force changes in the way the SATs are used or perhaps result in the ultimate abandonment of the tests completely. Frankly we hope the tests die, so that all the time and effort spent learning to take tests can be used in learning about a subject.

But they're not dead yet, and you must confront them. Even if the tests are probably nowhere near as important to your life as you may think they are—they can't be ignored entirely.

If you plan to go to college—any college—you will probably be required to submit SAT scores. This is a requirement even for schools that don't use the SATs as part of the admissions process and that may never look at the scores. Why not? The colleges get the test scores for free—you're the one who has to pay for the test.

Simply taking the test does have one advantage (we think it's an advantage anyway). It gets you on a lot of mailing lists, and you get literature from a bunch of colleges you might never have heard of. The Educational Testing Service sells lists of the names of college-bound students to different schools for recruiting purposes. In all the glossy advertising you receive you might just find out about a good school that you have never heard of before. It's a small compensation, but it's something.

Since you're going to be required to take the test anyway, you may just as well try to get a good score. If you're going for a selective college, the test score can influence admissions. Some scholarship aid is tied to test scores. Consideration for the prestigious National Merit Scholarship is based on PSAT scores. And there are more subtle advantages of scoring high. No matter how many times we tell you that the tests don't measure anything significant, no matter how many flaws and downright errors of the tests are pointed out by critics, no matter how many times you tell yourself, "I am not a test score," somewhere down deep you are going to feel a little better about yourself if you get a high score. If you blow it, there will be that tiny inner voice that keeps repeating "dummy, dummy!" The score will not only influence the college that chooses you, it will influence the colleges you will apply to. It shouldn't, but let's be realistic, you have had SATs knocked into your head for years. How could you possibly remain unaffected? It will also affect, however subtly, the way your parents, teachers, guidance counselors, and fellow students think about you.

If you go to an upper-middle-class school where most of the students are college bound, you probably have SAT courses as part of the regular curriculum. There are also coaching services available, as well as stores full of books on how to "beat" the SATs.

Unfortunately, many of the courses and books aren't really much help in raising your score. You get into memorizing long lists of words that will never appear on the tests. Sometimes this sort of study can make you more nervous, raise your anxiety, and thus lower your score.

USE THE GRAPEVINE

The best thing to do is ask around. Find out what others are doing. In some areas kids are very sophisticated about getting ready for tests. Remember you're not trying to catch up on years of education in a few weeks or months. All you're trying to do is find the best technique for beating the test.

If you don't have a good grapevine for test-beating information in your area, or if you simply can't afford $500 for a test-beating course, then your best bet is to get some books that have old SATs in them. Become as familiar as you can with the tests. But don't become obsessed by them.

While you should use any honest gimmick you can to get a higher score—don't cheat. The security on SATs is often lax, but if you do get caught with a calculator, or worse with a stolen exam, you can be in big trouble. Cheating is absolutely not worth the chance you take. A lousy score won't hurt you one-tenth as much as a charge of cheating.

Keep the tests in perspective. Remember, they are not nearly as significant as you think they are. Don't think you're dumber than someone else just because the other person got higher SAT scores. Conversely, don't think you're smarter because you got the higher score. SAT scores, said one critic of the tests, are not something engraved inside your skull. Test scores are not the sort of thing to compete over—some competition is inevitable—but keep it at a minimum.

Don't let the scores keep you from going for a college

you really want to attend. If there is a school you think would be right for you, but your SATs fall below the averages for the entering class listed in the college guide, don't give up. Remember tests are only part of the selection process, even for the most selective schools. On the other hand, don't be surprised or crushed if that highly desirable school rejects you and accepts someone you know who had lower scores. Perhaps he or she had other qualities that the school was looking for.

Don't compete over test scores. It's just not worth the effort.

• 5 •
THE CHOSEN ONES

From the time Samantha ("Sam") got into the ninth grade, her whole life revolved around getting into an Ivy League college. Sam grew up in a wealthy New York City suburb where parents were high achievers who expected the same of their kids. Sam's father was an executive with IBM. He had graduated from a state school, and he wanted to see his children do even better. He believed that if Sam went to an Ivy League school she would have a head start on a career and earn a lot of money. Sam's mother had graduated from a small liberal arts college in the Midwest. Successful daughters make mothers look good, and she equated Princeton with success. Besides, if a girl went to an Ivy League school, she might marry a boy going to an Ivy League school and that would be an added plus in security and prestige.

Samantha was a tough competitor. A leading member of the track team, she was editor of the high school newspaper, twelfth in her class, and one of those elected to sing at Area All-State Chorus. In her senior year when the other students in accelerated courses were clawing and tearing at each other to pick up every extra point, Sam joined right in. Like many people she would tell herself she wasn't really competing with others, only with herself.

But deep down she knew better. Sam really believed that people who get into high-powered schools are better than others and that those who work hard and prove themselves invariably do get in.

Just saying the names Harvard and Yale fired Sam's imagination. Not that she knew anything about these schools or any other schools. For all her drive and ambition Samantha had absolutely no conception of what college was like. She was an only child, so she didn't have brothers or sisters away at school. There was no major college nearby. Because she had no clear idea of what college would be like, she exaggerated what it would do for her, convinced that the school she chose would define her life. She would quite literally be a different person if she went to Harvard from what she'd be if she went to Stanford.

When Sam thought of Stanford, she pictured herself jogging in a blaze of West Coast sunlight, healthy, athletic, surrounded by plants, and eating Granola bars. This Sam was smart but outdoorsy. When she thought of Harvard, she was a shy, intellectual, intense Sam going to school in a gray castle on a cloud, which gave out degrees made of fourteen-karat gold.

Pursuing admission to an Ivy League school did not come without pain. Though Samantha was a hard worker with plenty of self-discipline, she took a lot of courses that bored her just because they looked good on her record. She didn't stint when it came to studying, though the content of the courses meant nothing to her. She worked solely for grades. Her intense competitiveness got in the way of friendships. Everybody at school was a potential rival.

Sam approached extracurricular activities in the same way she did her classes. She didn't like to sing, but she stuck with chorus for four years just because it would look good on her high school record. To try and raise her already high SAT scores, she spent hours in the library memorizing vocabulary lists instead of reading novels. When it came to track she kept pushing herself to become a better runner, but no matter how fast she ran, it was never good enough.

By the fall of her senior year the pressures to get into a prestigious college were brutal. Nobody in the upper third of Sam's class would admit which colleges they were applying to. Never let the enemy know what you're up to. Then the wild rumors started. Somebody knew somebody who got into Yale because his grandfather phoned the admissions department on his deathbed, begged that his grandson be admitted, and donated a fortune to the school. When Yale let his grandson in, the old man gasped thank you and died happy. Somebody else knew somebody who knew somebody who had mediocre marks but who worked for a candy company. This guy got into Harvard because he sent the admissions committee a big piece of chocolate in the shape of the Harvard seal. The chocolate was accompanied by an essay describing life as bittersweet. This story, which everyone believed, sent shock waves through the senior class.

Everybody, Sam included, spied on everybody else. The valedictorian of the class found out the class rank of every student and was using this information to take cheap shots at the rest of the class. People were said to be cheating on tests. It was rumored that the president of the class had bribed kids to vote for him because holding a class office would be a plus on his college application form. Somebody had supposedly discovered a way of beating the system by applying to three top universities as an English major since there weren't many English majors in the class. Once into an Ivy League school, she'd switch to premed or business.

All around Sam people were buying college guides by the bunch arguing over which was best, *Fiske* or *Barron's*, and checking to see which schools had the highest ratings. College catalogs, bright and glossy, were piling up in bedrooms, on the floor of living rooms, even on kitchen tables. Everybody was going crazy filling out applications and writing essays, which they hoped sounded both lively and profound.

TRAUMA WEEK

The process wasn't made any easier with parents hanging over kids, phoning schools, bothering guidance counselors. In December word came in about early decisions applicants. Most applicants were deferred until regular admissions, and class tensions grew worse. By March the senior class was running scared. The second week of April, when schools sent out acceptances and rejections, was aptly dubbed trauma week, and trauma it was. Still, Sam, who was proud of her achievements, felt confident. She was convinced she'd make it. She had played the college entrance game by the rules and played it well. It had been a grueling year, but admission to one of the Ivies would make it all worth while.

The fatal mail delivery arrived on April 13. Sam tore open the half dozen thin envelopes that reached her house that day. All were from Ivy League schools. Each was a rejection. Acceptances come in fat envelopes stuffed with additional information. Rejections come in thin ones.

What else is there to say? Stunned, shocked, devastated, Sam looked at her mother and said "So much for trying." The college application process was the first real failure of her life.

TEENAGE COMPETITION

This might be a good moment to give Sam some much needed privacy and take a look at how she could have handled competing for admission to college in a more constructive way. To begin with, it would have been useful to keep things in perspective. Highly competitive people like Sam often develop tunnel vision just at the moment when they need to keep a balanced view. Getting into the Ivies doesn't mean automatic success. Not getting in doesn't mean automatic failure. Life just isn't that simple.

The number of teens caught up in the race for the Ivies is rather small. Most people don't think very much about them one way or the other, don't apply to them, and don't go through life wishing they had a closetful of T-shirts that say Princeton instead of Kansas, FSU, or wherever. Most students attend state schools, choose colleges with campuses located fairly close to where they live, or commute to a school an easy bus ride or drive from their house. Granted the Ivies are prestigious schools with definite advantages, but advantages exist elsewhere. Many highly successful people have never gone near an Ivy League school and couldn't find one on a map.

It might have helped Sam to keep a clearer eye on the odds. The children of alumni often number as high as 25 percent, one-quarter of the entering class at a high-powered school. There are just too many hard-working students with high grades and impressive extracurricular credentials vying to get into the remaining slots for the selection process to be even remotely fair. While the admissions staff of a college is generally made up of ordinary human beings doing the best they can, they are not all-seeing. They do not have magic powers. They make mistakes. Qualified students applying to an Ivy League school are playing a game that's as fluky as playing the lottery. There is a difference. Usually when people don't win lotteries they feel disappointed but they don't feel like personal failures.

Sam was so bruised by the rejections she received from the Ivies that she couldn't face any further competition during senior year and flunked a phys. ed. course. Her teachers howled. Her parents moaned. But Sam was really just retrenching, taking a step backward, which helped her take a giant step forward toward growing up. She was beginning to ask basic questions, define her goals, determining when and where she wanted to compete. In the end she decided to attend a fine small liberal arts college. Once there she took a history course just because she was interested in the subject. She also took a course in pottery making, focusing on the pleasure of creating something she liked instead of trying to be the best artist in the class. The class was friendly and relaxed, and she got to know some nice people. She began to feel proud of herself again, pleased with the good marks she'd earned in high school, pleased with her prowess as a runner. She liked her college, maybe liked it a lot more than she would have liked Harvard.

THE HOT COLLEGES

Wesley Kim wasn't interested in attending an Ivy. He had his heart set on a hot college. So did a lot of other students at the private school Wes went to. Like the Ivies hot colleges draw many more applicants than there are openings. It's hard to know why some schools are more popular than others. Sometimes it's merely a pretty campus, a good basketball team, or being near a good ski slope or a sunny stretch of beach.

Wes's parents, who were from Korea, set a high value on education. They had made great financial sacrifices to send him to a private high school. For years Wes had heard that the only way he could repay them was through academic success. Even getting the freedom to go out on Saturday nights was a struggle for Wes. His parents felt he should stay home and study. Besides parental pressure, Wes, like Sam, faced peer pressure. The senior class at his school was obsessed with getting into the "right" college. It was "step on anyone who gets in your way" and "every student for himself." When Wes's best friends talked about how scared they were that they'd be rejected from the schools of their choice, Wes started avoiding them. He kept his feelings bottled up inside because he didn't dare talk to the very people he was competing with. When your goal is to win for the sake of winning and to beat out everyone else, life can become very lonely.

When Wes received his first rejection, he burst into tears. Next day school was tough. He broke through the wall of isolation he'd built for himself and told his best friend about his rejection. His best friend told others. People either felt sorry for Wes or pretended to feel sorry for him while secretly feeling relieved that there was one less person in the running for that particular school. At home Wes's parents were understanding, but he sensed their disappointment. It was a tough burden to carry.

What made the situation so unfair was watching other students who had lower grades get into the school he wanted. He asked himself if being Korean had hurt him. There were so many Asian-American students applying to colleges these days. On the surface Wes seemed to be bearing up well, but underneath he was angry and hurt, searching around for someone or something to blame.

Because Wes had put so much effort into applying to a few hot colleges and so little effort into checking out other options, he wound up commuting to a nearby school that he didn't want to go to. It was his safety school, one he assumed from the start he could get into. Wes told himself he would transfer into a hot college as soon as he could.

Wes should have kept his priorities straight. Checking out safe schools is important. Had he put aside his pursuit of a dream school for a while, he would have had time to search for a school he could both get into and like. It might also have reassured Wes to remember that fads come and go. The safe school he's embarrassed to attend today may be the hot college of tomorrow.

NOT MAKING IT

If Sam made it to a non-Ivy she liked and Wes made it to a college he could live with, Tom didn't make it to college at all. He had always had trouble competing and by senior year was too overwhelmed to try. Tom went to a competitive high school where he earned about a "C" average. This drove his parents crazy. They were always at him, nagging him to do his homework, accusing him of destroying his life. At wine-and-cheese parties where other parents bragged about their children's scholastic achievements Tom's parents were stuck with saying nothing in reply or changing the subject, or so it seemed to Tom. He often asked himself if his parents really cared about him. He was quite convinced they would have traded him in for a computer if the computer would get straight "A's."

Not surprisingly senior year brought Tom a strong dose of senioritis. He was bored with his classes, anxious about the future, and depressed and frightened by the frenzied race to get into college he saw going on around him. His marks dropped further. He postponed sending in applications to colleges, telling himself he had plenty of time. Besides, he was sure he wouldn't get into a good school anyway, so why bother with anything less? Rejections from any school would provide his parents with yet another excuse to turn on him.

So Tom spent his spring term surfing with his friend Jim, who had applied to several top colleges and was so crushed when he was rejected that he was now in therapy, and with Ted who was debating whether to join the army or get a job after graduation. By summer Tom figured he'd take a year off school and just travel around picking up work as best he could. Why bother with college at all? Why bother competing when, as he told himself, he'd only lose?

Obviously Tom is under so much pressure he can't see his own strengths. Despite his parents' attitude, a "C" average is far from disastrous, especially since he attended a tough high school. If he had the self-confidence to try, he could get into any number of schools. There are even schools that accept virtually all their applicants, and that doesn't make them poor colleges. A school with a supportive atmosphere that could provide Tom with a chance to get away from home, discover new interests, and meet new people might work wonders for him.

MAKING IT BIG

So far we've talked about compromise and learning to take rejection. These are important aspects of competition. But so is achieving your aim. If you don't try, you can never make it, and if you do, well sometimes as with Jennifer, you do come out on top.

Jennifer was twenty-fourth in her class. Yet she was accepted at Harvard. The valedictorian of the class wasn't. Jennifer attributed her success to a rare combination of factors. She played basketball and the viola. Maybe Harvard just needed a tall female viola player this year. Whatever the reasons for her getting in, Jennifer was ecstatic. She wrote everyone she knew to tell them the good news. Her best friend predicted she would next go through phone books starting with the letter A to let every stranger in the county know she'd been accepted to Harvard.

Jennifer was the envy of her senior class, and though she had to put up with veiled insults and grumbling, it is easier to be on the receiving end of jealousy than the other way round. Yet even Jennifer was distressed when she was rejected from Cornell, Princeton, and Yale. She asked herself if Harvard had made a mistake taking her. But these self-doubts didn't last long, and soon she was euphoric again. Why not? Somebody's got to win the brass ring on the merry-go-round, and if it happens to be you, enjoy it.

Maybe the person who handled the competitive pressures of getting into college best was Samantha's friend Leon, who went to her high school. Second in his class and deeply interested in science, he confidently applied to ten as he put it "designer schools" with outstanding scientific programs and advanced technological equipment. Though he was subjected to the same excruciating agony as every other college-bound senior in his class, he spent as much waiting time as he could reading science fiction to escape. He did not compete academically just to clobber everybody else. Actually he hated seeing classes deteriorate. Once they'd provided learning experiences. Now they were battlegrounds for grades. He refused to join extra-curricular activities that bored him just so they'd show up on his high school record.

When December rolled around, Leon learned he had been deferred at Princeton. Next day school was miserable. Leon kept asking himself why he wasn't accepted. He asked himself if maybe he should have joined some extra-curricular activities after all. But he reminded himself that he was an excellent student and a hard worker and that he had many more colleges to hear from. Only a few days later he learned that he was accepted to the Massachusetts Institute of Technology and that gave him a boost of optimism. He realized that he could get into a top school.

After a mix of acceptances and rejections Leon chose Stanford. Not only was it a superb school academically, but he felt comfortable there. He realized that he would still be the same person wherever he was and no place would be problem free. Things might or might not work out at Stanford, but the school gave him a lot to look forward to. Science at Stanford would be a challenge. Leon notified Stanford that he'd be attending in the fall and spent the evening burning all his other college catalogs in the fireplace.

EASING THE PRESSURE

Everyone can't be as academically gifted as Leon. Everyone can't be as lucky as Jennifer. But wherever you are in the college-search process, if you feel as if you're looking down the barrel of a gun, let's sum up the ways you can ease the competitive stresses.

First, keep things in perspective. Choosing a college is an important decision, but it isn't a matter of life and death. You will still be the same person wherever you go. If you believe you could put things into perspective if only your parents would stop pushing you so hard to compete, try to talk to them. Maybe if they realize they're contributing to the problem rather than helping with the solution, they'll cool down. If peer pressure's getting to you, try to distance yourself from the rest of your class. Okay, that isn't easy, but senior year is a special time when teenagers have one foot in high school and one foot in the outside world. Use the situation to your advantage.

Get a part-time job if you don't already have one. Try to meet new people, preferably high school graduates. Broadening your horizons will show you that the whole world is not caught up in the college-search obsession. If nothing else, at least part of your day will be spent away from people scaring each other to death with horror stories that make college admissions officers sound like werewolves.

Expand your selection of schools. By all means apply to a few dream schools, Ivies, or hot colleges. But don't just choose schools because they're given a high rating in a guide book. Focus on your own needs. When you apply to a highly competitive school, look at it as a long shot. Don't count on being accepted. Try to stay a bit detached. It may even be wise to skip a guided tour of the campus. Accept that you will be disappointed if you are not accepted, but don't look upon the rejection as a personal failure. Everybody runs into rejection sooner or later, and only if you can handle it, can you pull yourself together and compete again.

Consider schools your friends haven't thought of. There are all kinds of interesting little colleges, women's schools, large universities with varied programs. Instead of constantly drifting off into fantasies about the Ivies, expend a few fantasies on safe schools. After all, even if it's not your first choice, it helps if you like whatever school you may attend. You'll be a better student no matter where you go if you arrive with some enthusiasm.

Follow your instincts. If you have a particular hobby, say music, check out schools with strong extracurricular music programs. Would you like to go to college in a hot climate? A cold climate? Would you like to spend four years in an exciting city like New Orleans, a cultural mecca like New York, a city full of college students like Boston? Would you prefer a school where sports are big or nonexistent? If you want to meet many different kinds of people, a large state school might be the best place for you. If you live in Maine, go to school in Texas. If you live in Texas, go to school in Maine. It'd be a change, and after all, change, growth, and new adventures are an important part of the college experience. Look, if you love animals, going to school in a city with a great zoo might be fun.

Don't let competitive pressures fool you into a choice you are not comfortable with.

Try to remember that entering a college does not involve signing a pact in blood. You can change majors, you can change colleges. Lots of people do. You might even be able to reapply successfully to one of the colleges that rejected you first time around.

• 6 •
HOW YOU PLAY THE GAME

At the first Little League game we ever attended there was a big sign posted at the field. It read: "Remember They Are Only Kids." That afternoon there were a lot of people who couldn't follow the simple instruction.

As with most Little League games the spectators were mostly parents or other relatives. They naturally cheered their own children and their children's team. That was fine. But some could become downright abusive to members of the opposing team.

We particularly remember one fellow in his mid-thirties. He had picked out an overweight player on the opposing team for special attention. Every time this kid came to bat, the guy would yell, "Get that fat slob! He can't hit anything!"

When the kid actually did hit the ball, he was thrown out easily at first.

"He's too fat to run!" yelled the guy in the audience.

We remind you that we were not sitting in Yankee Stadium. It was a small field. The kid at bat could hear every word that was being shouted. You could actually see him wince. He may have been all of eleven years old.

On the field the coaches were not images of calm, wise, and caring adults. These fellows did a lot of screaming and hand waving. One pitcher who had just given up a couple of runs left the mound in tears after what appeared to be a bawling out by his angry coach.

We were told by those who attended these games regularly that this was a fairly typical game, but sometimes the parents got pretty bad—particularly when they had been drinking.

We do not wish to overdramatize this incident. Most of the parents in the stands behaved well, cheering both sides when there was a particularly good play, at least refraining from abuse. The coaches who were all volunteers were excitable and involved, but not, as far as we could tell, brutal. The winners certainly enjoyed the game, and the losers while dejected were not crushed. They would come back to play, and probably win, another day. Sports are about winning and losing.

We recount this incident merely to show how early sports competition starts in the United States and how intense it can become. There is no area in American life where competition is more intense and more naked than in sports. Organized competition begins in grade school and for most reaches its peak during the high school years. Very few become professional athletes. Even in colleges, sports have become increasingly professionalized. Most college students participate only as spectators.

A friend, a middle-aged newspaper reporter, recounted an experience he had. He was doing a nostalgia piece on his old high school. As part of his research he attended a football reunion banquet. All of the old high school football players, or as many who were still around and still cared, gathered to eat, drink, and talk about old times. Our friend had never been a football player. Indeed, in high school he had not been athletic at all, a situation that caused him no little pain at the time. But that was almost thirty years ago. Now he was meeting all his old classmates, shaking hands and slapping backs. None of them was in shape to play football anymore. They looked worse than he did.

At one point, near the end of the banquet, everyone in the audience was to stand, one by one, and announce his name and the years he had played on the old school team. The reporter who had never played was undecided. Would he simply remain in his seat, or would he stand up and make some witty comment? As the standees drew nearer and nearer to the table at which he sat, the reporter was suddenly gripped by panic, even though he was there in a professional capacity, to report on the event. All sorts of old feelings of inadequacy and shame that he had not felt since his high school days suddenly rose up. Before the turn came for people at his table to stand, he made a lame excuse and ran from the room. Some old wounds still hurt now and then.

WINNING IS EVERYTHING

It's often been said that the United States is a nation obsessed by sports. That's true enough, but this country is not the only nation to have such an obsession. The ancient Greeks honored their athletes above practically anyone else. The spectator sports of the Romans were brutal, but immensely popular. Games in British public schools of the last century were generally thought to be more important than studies. Both contemporary China and the Soviet Union have enormous sports programs. We once saw a program on the training of the Japanese women's Olympic volley ball team. The intensity of the training was almost terrifying. So the United States isn't the only nation to be obsessed by sports. But it's right up there.

The dominant philosophy in sports today is the one popularized by the professional football coach Vince Lombardi—it holds that winning is everything. Lombardi never actually advocated cheating, but simply winning at practically any cost was so important that it shoved out all notions of good sportsmanship and fair play. Indeed the "winning is the only thing" philosophy is common throughout American society at large today.

At one time in American amateur athletics, there was at least lip service paid to the old saying, "It doesn't matter whether you win or lose but how you play the game." We can remember that saying used when we went to high school. Very few of us believed it at the time, but at least no one laughed. Can you imagine your high school football coach going up in front of the team before a big game and telling them it didn't matter whether they won or lost! The team would probably think that what he had lost was his mind. All the talk about having played well is saved until after the game. That's what losers talk about. It's regarded an excuse and a rationalization. For many people involved in sports, even high school sports, winning is the only thing. This is particularly true in the highly publicized sports like football and basketball.

One high school football coach gained a certain amount of national notoriety by biting the head off a live frog during a pregame pep talk to his team. The action was an extreme one to be sure, but there is generally a lot of shouting about crushing, pulverizing, and smashing the opponents.

Brian

Brian grew up in a small town with a championship football team. The volunteer fire department raised money for the team. The Veterans of Foreign Wars raised money for the team. Watching the Saturday afternoon high school football game was the major form of recreation in the town. Men in their forties and fifties still went to see the games and cheer on their old high school team. Every year there was an annual football awards banquet, and these same men went to that to cheer on young athletes and to reminisce about the good old days.

Growing up in an atmosphere like this, most boys wanted to play football and most fathers wanted their sons to play. Brian and his father were big sports fans. There weren't many good jobs in Brian's town. One by one the factories were closing. Classes were overcrowded at the local high school, and academics were weak. Nobody came to the academic awards assemblies if they could possibly help it. Athletic awards assemblies were well attended, and pep rallies were a big hit. So if a boy dreamed of getting out of town and going to college, he thought first of trying to win a football scholarship.

Brian joined Pop Warner football when he was in fifth grade, but though he was strong and muscular, he was short. He knew early on that he'd never make it to the varsity team in high school, so he switched to the second most popular sport in town, wrestling. The town had produced an Olympic gold medal winner in wrestling who had gotten his early training in the high school sports program. Brian was inspired to follow in his footsteps. Still, even though wrestlers were respected, he couldn't shake off the feeling he was a second-class citizen because he didn't play football. The football coach was the highest-paid coach on the high school staff. He made it clear that he thought football was the only sport that mattered.

Football players were the superheroes of the school. Girls loved to wear football jerseys and go out with football players. But if Brian resented and envied the football team, at least wrestlers were better off than soccer players. The soccer team rarely won its games. The school put little money and effort into building a soccer program, and the football coach enjoyed telling his boys, the football players, that the soccer team was full of faggots. But at least soccer was a team sport. The ski team, which was really based on individual competition, wasn't taken seriously, and the tennis team couldn't even get its winners' pictures in the town newspaper. The skiiers and tennis players, who were usually richer than the football players and wrestlers, insisted they were really scholar athletes. They sneered at the football players and called them dumb jocks. The football players and wrestlers called them nerds, and worse.

Even though wrestling wasn't a team sport in the same sense as baseball, basketball, football, or soccer, it was certainly a tough contact sport requiring formidable strength, agility, and endurance. Wrestling is a popular high school sport because it allows individuals to compete within their own weight class. Thus no one is too small or too big. High school and college wrestling has nothing to do with professional wrestling, which is entertainment, not a sport.

Brian gave wrestling his all. The coach, Brian's parents, and his fellow team members kept him under constant pressure. He would do anything to qualify for a match. Sometimes he had to lose as much as eight pounds in a day. Drained, tired, and thirsty, he would race madly up and down in front of the school boiler while wrapped in a plastic suit in order to sweat off pounds. When he reached home starving and miserable, there was his family eating dinner. He had to smell the delicious scent of food cooking. It was unbearable. Usually he wound up snarling at his sister and slamming the door to his room shut.

To wrestle his way onto the team, he'd psyche himself up to hate his opponent and take it out on him on the mat. Of course, once he got the spot, the anger vanished most of the time. But sometimes if the competition was especially keen, whoever lost stayed angry and said a lot of unpleasant things about the winner behind his back. Once the high school team went up against teams from other schools all the intergroup rivalry ceased. Now rivalry was directed totally at the other team, and everybody on Brian's team pulled for each other.

Tournaments were an ordeal. To prepare for them the wrestling team was put through grueling physical punishment including three-minute handstands against the gym wall. Wrestling took concentration and determination, and it gave Brian personal pride. But it wasn't fun. Once he was hospitalized for a concussion. Even when things were going well, wrestling season was a long four and a half months without relaxation or escape. Brian had nightmares over wrestling, waking up in terror dreaming he'd lost.

In Brian's last year in high school he prayed he would make it to the all-state tournament. Colleges scout you when you reach all-state. But first he had to make it to regionals where top winners from different counties compete.

Brian's big match was held in the gym at the other school. The intensity was fantastic. The gym was packed. Everything felt different to Brian; even the lights seemed brighter than usual. Everybody was screaming and he couldn't think. He felt as if he had to win this one match. His whole future was on the line. When he went up against his opponent, he forced himself to be disciplined and keep his emotions under control but he was in a murderous rage. When he stepped forward, he was booed by the fans from the other school. Well, what could you expect? Everyone in Brian's school knew that the other school was full of cheaters who'd stoop to anything and any distraction to win.

Brian was on the verge of taking the match when suddenly everything went wrong and he was pinned. To his humiliation he burst into tears. Nothing in his life had ever felt worse than this loss. Now there would be no state tournament, no glory, no scholarship. After the match the fans went wild, and kids from Brian's high school ran through the halls tearing down posters and kicking lockers. There was almost a fight among the wrestlers, but Brian and his teammates were hustled off to their bus fast. No one was hurt, there was no major damage, but it was an ugly moment.

That spring Brian went out for track. He didn't win, but he had a good time. He enjoyed track for its own sake. It was just something to do. Brian had decided to enroll in the local community college in the fall. The school had a decent accounting program, and by living at home and working part-time, he'd make enough money to transfer to the main four-year branch of the state college in a couple of years. He would play soccer at community college, but he wouldn't go out for wrestling. Too intense. He would never lose interest in sports, and he would always remember wrestling as one of the most exciting and challenging experiences of his life, but from now on, athletics was for recreation only, a hobby and a diversion.

Brian's experience is a fairly common one. The competitive pressures of high school sports, even relatively minor sports like wrestling, can be agonizingly intense. Brian handled the pressure in the best way he possibly could. He threw himself completely into the competition, but in the end he discovered that he didn't really want to put so much of his life into sports. He would, however, always be able to look back on what he had accomplished with great pride. Sports were, in a very real sense, a character builder for him.

IT'S DIFFERENT FOR GIRLS

Traditionally girls' athletics in high school has not been taken very seriously. The boys were the athletes, the girls the cheerleaders. There were certain sports, like field hockey, that were reserved for girls. But there was no real competition. No one, outside of those who were on the team, really cared.

A lot of that has changed. At one time it was assumed that women couldn't even run a marathon. Now women regularly run the marathon in times that would have been records for men twenty years ago. In sports like gymnastics and tennis, both physically demanding, the women often are more famous than the men. Twenty years ago Americans derided women athletes from Eastern Europe as being "unfeminine" and "too muscular." Now muscles are "in" for American women. Women pumping iron—unthinkable for most a decade ago—is a popular and accepted activity, particularly for young women.

But the millennium of absolute athletic equality for women in high school has not yet arrived. Girls' teams are generally underfunded and often ignored. Attempts by girls to join their high school baseball or even football teams are rare enough to make news. Such attempts usually inspire derision and sometimes panic among male coaches and players and are regarded as attacks on their masculinity.

The fact that athletics for girls is still not taken too seriously in the vast majority of high schools can be a real advantage for the nonathletic or noncompetitive girl. She doesn't have to compete, and unlike the nonathletic boy, no one is going to call her names. It is the really athletic high school girl who still runs up against the old and ingrained sexual stereotypes. That can make the competition doubly difficult.

Barbara

In fifth grade Barbara had written a story about a little girl who wanted to play football. It was a sad wistful story because it was really about Barbara herself. She was a naturally gifted athlete, happier playing football informally with her brother and his friends than just hanging around with the girls.

Her parents steered her toward girls' softball, explaining that for a girl playing football was the impossible dream. Barbara was angry and perplexed, but she was good at softball, so she kept playing.

By her sophomore year in high school, Barbara was the school's star pitcher, no small achievement especially since the girls' softball team won the district championship that year.

Athletes at Barbara's school were given respect and even special treatment. Barbara took full advantage of her perks. Though Barbara was a reasonably good student, she skipped tests and cut classes occasionally, knowing she could get away with it. When she was caught smoking in the girls' bathroom, she got a reprimand instead of being suspended from the team. When she was caught drinking, she was kept off the team for a few weeks. Anyone else would have been off for the entire season. At least that's what most kids believed.

Then the blow fell; Barbara never knew how the rumor began. Was it started by someone who resented her success? By a competitor who wanted to be pitcher? Was she just so well known at school she'd become a target? The rumor reached Barbara in the form of a sign someone stuck in her locker showing her in her softball uniform looking just like a boy. Someone had written "dike" across the front.

Barbara was horribly upset. She was almost too shaken to go to practice. She debated telling the coach about what had happened, but she couldn't face talking about it to anyone. She even asked herself if she should quit the team. How could she? Why should she? Sports was her whole life.

She had put so much into softball. She hadn't dared to tell people her deepest longing, to pitch in the major leagues. Everybody would just laugh. For years she'd known that the athletic scholarship she would receive one day (and there was no doubt about it, she would) could at best lead to a job as a coach or a phys. ed. instructor. That's all a girl could do in team sports. There were no big leagues ahead for her. And now this rumor that she was a lesbian. She felt attacked on all sides. Barbara lost her next game. It was her first loss that season, and it made her want to quit school or run away from home. Barbara did neither. She hung in there and became the best pitcher the school's girls' softball team ever had. She received some recognition for this accomplishment. But there is no real happy ending to the story. She never got anywhere near the acclaim that she would have received had she been a boy. And the rumors about her sexual orientation continued to haunt her. Her experience might well discourage any other talented girl athlete in the school.

Do you have any exceptional girl athletes in your school?

If you do, think for a moment about what the general attitude is toward them. Do they get the same sort of respect that the boys get? Somehow we doubt it.

SPORTS—A WAY UP

Practically everyone who has ever played sports in high school, and a lot who haven't, at one time or another have dreamed about pitching in the Houston Astrodome, Busch Stadium, Fenway Park, or Shea Stadium or fantasized about playing in the NFL. But we quickly realize that it is a fantasy, and active sports become an enjoyable, but distinctly minor, part of life. However, for some, sports represent a slim, but real chance to get something that life might not otherwise have offered.

Donald was black, and like a lot of black kids in a big city school he dreamed of playing professional basketball. But he wasn't tall enough or good enough. If he was anything, it was fast, the most talented person ever to hit his school track team.

Donald, though he was very bright, had no interest in the academic side of school. He couldn't see the point of classes and studying. The school he went to was overcrowded, and somewhere along the line he'd been tracked into the "dummy" group as the kids called it. The school administrators alternated between threatening Donald and cajoling him to get him to do his work. One year they refused to allow him to attend a major track meet. Incensed, Donald's father went to school to argue with the principal about the decision. He insisted that Donald's future was riding on his getting an athletic scholarship, and if he wasn't allowed to attend important meets, he'd never qualify. The principal insisted that Donald wouldn't get a scholarship anywhere unless he raised his marks.

But in Donald's senior year after a particularly spectacular win he did get offered a scholarship, a full scholarship to a prestigious university. It was the talk of the school. Most of the white kids hated Donald for getting the scholarship. The class valedictorian was furious because she couldn't even get into that school. The principal was embarrassed and the teachers resentful. Many in the high school complained about corruption and about "some people getting special treatment." Reactions among the black students were mixed. Most thought it a good opportunity and urged Donald to take the scholarship.

But Donald wasn't convinced. This wasn't like a basketball scholarship leading to the NBA. He had to consider what kind of work he'd be doing in four years. He didn't want to go to a school where practically everybody was white and where the academic competition was fierce. He wasn't even sure he wanted to go to college at all. He really didn't like school. But as his father reminded him, he wouldn't much like working at the local supermarket for the rest of his life either, and that's where he'd be without college.

Then came the news that Donald was offered an athletic scholarship to a nonprestigious college in a major urban area with a large black student population. The academic competition would be nowhere near as tough as at the fancy elite school. There would be other students from the bottom half of their high school graduating class. After thinking things through, Donald decided that he would definitely turn down the offer from the famous university. Some people thought he was crazy. But he really believed he needed to be someplace he could handle where he'd be comfortable. Otherwise he might drop out or never get a degree; that's what happens to many kids who get athletic scholarships. Donald went off to school in the fall feeling optimistic. He was ready to work a lot harder in college than he had in high school, and he was convinced he'd make it. He was delighted that his athletic prowess had won him that chance.

"NO PASS, NO PLAY"

In a lot of schools the general feeling is "the jocks get it all." They get the prestige, they get the girls, and a lot of them like Donald even get a free ride to college with athletic scholarships. But over the last few years a revolution of sorts has been brewing against the jocks.

There has been much criticism of American education. It has been called mediocre and worse. There have been horror stories about kids who graduate from high school who can barely read. There are widespread fears that our educational system is too easygoing and that we are falling behind the Japanese and others who study like crazy when they're in high school.

A lot of the criticism has focused on athletics. In the eyes of the critics, too much emphasis has been placed on athletics and not enough on academics. The result of this criticism has been a whole flock of new rules about who can play and who can't. The rules vary greatly from school to school, but they have generally been lumped under the heading of "No Pass, No Play." Sometimes they come as a real shocker.

Kerry was an average student and an above average football player. Football had always been a big deal at Kerry's school, which had a long winning tradition. The 1985 season was one of the best, the school team, the Tigers won the regional championship. A good part of the team's success was due to Kerry's speed and skill as a running back. He was only a junior, and he was looking forward to a great senior year.

During 1985 however, his school had adopted a "No Pass, No Play" rule. The rule held that if you were flunking a course, you couldn't participate in any extracurricular activities until you got a passing grade. That meant any time you flunked you were barred from activities for at least one full marking period. The school always had academic eligibility rules, but there were a million ways to get around them. The new policy was tough—there were to be no exceptions.

The first year the policy was in effect a couple of football players were benched, but they were second stringers, and it didn't make much difference. The second year Kerry flunked physics, and he was barred right at the beginning of the football season. Ken, a first string center, was also dropped, and a few other players actually quit the team because their parents insisted that practice was taking too much time and energy away from their schoolwork. The team was devastated. There would be no regional championship for the Tigers that year. There was a lot of anger against the administrators who had put in the "No Pass, No Play" rule.

Kerry was personally crushed. Being a football star had given him a feeling of pride and self-esteem. He came from a poor family, and he had never been a very good student. Football gave him a chance to excel; people noticed him. Sure, Kerry knew that he was not going to make it in the NFL. He knew that he wasn't even going to get a chance to go to one of the big football colleges. But he figured that football would get him a scholarship to one of the smaller schools. In fact, it was his desire to go to college that got him in trouble with grades in the first place. He took a physics course because he figured he'd need it to get into college. That's the course he flunked, and that's what kept him off the team. If he had no plans to go to college, he never would have taken physics in the first place. He would have stuck with the courses that he could pass easily, and he would have been able to play football.

Kerry was bitter. So was his father who had been a star on the Tigers when he had gone to high school. They both felt the "No Pass, No Play" rule had been forced on the school by newcomers who were snobbish about education and who didn't understand what sports meant to the school and to the kids who played them.

Kerry's dilemma raises some tough issues that are going to come up again and again in schools all over the country in the next few years. You may already have the equivalent of a "No Pass, No Play" rule in your school, or the school administration may be considering one.

Obviously the main goal of any school is education. Sports are secondary. If practicing and playing on a team takes so much time away from schoolwork that a student is in serious academic trouble, then it's sports that have to give way.

Moreover, regulations like the "No Pass, No Play" rule signal that sports have simply become too important in many schools and that the whole emphasis has to be changed. Being good in sports is just fine, but classroom work must come first.

All of the old talk of learning "sportsmanship" and "teamwork" and "building character" is gone. School sports, particularly the high-profile team sports like football, are now recognized as being about competing and winning. What many educators are saying is that winning on the field is nowhere near as important as winning in the classroom.

Opponents of the tough new rules contend that they are discriminatory and often rob poor and minority students of a chance to further their education with athletic scholarships. Supporters of the rules point out that only a tiny percentage of high school athletes ever make it into professional sports. All the rest are going to need other skills once they get out of school. To allow anyone to believe that he or she is going to be able to get through life by being a top-notch high school athlete is a cruel hoax, they say.

Will tough new rules about who can and cannot participate in high school athletics really change the way things are done? Or in schools where athletics has traditionally been a high priority will such rules merely spawn new ways of avoiding the academic standards? In the future will students like Kerry automatically take snap courses? Will teachers be pressured to pass promising athletes no matter how poorly they do in class?

More significantly, will the rules change the attitudes of students—will they change your attitude? Is the good student going to be admired, respected, and envied the way a varsity football player is?

On a more personal level, will the rules encourage athletes to take their studies more seriously. Or will it simply discourage many of them and make them feel that there is nothing in school that is worth while. For many, athletics has been the primary way, sometimes the only way, that they have been able to gain self-esteem. Keeping them off the team may not make them better students. Indeed, it may result in their dropping out of school entirely.

These are tough issues. We don't have any easy answers, besides a general feeling that it is a good idea to promote academic performance. But school administrators had better be darned sure that is what their policy is really accomplishing. They'd better be sure it's not just punishing students who happen to be good athletes but are not good in school or it's not just rewarding schools that are willing to bend and overlook the rules.

The jury is still out on this one.

•7•

"AND EVERYTHING NICE"

Terri said no to a date for the prom because she found out that the boy who asked her had asked somebody else first. Terri didn't want to be anybody's second choice. Laurel was first in her class until she reached junior high. Then she joined football cheerleaders, made it to the "top" clique, and decided popularity was a lot more important than grades. By eighth grade she was off the honor roll. Michelle had no friends and thought of herself as the class freak until her freshman year of high school. Then she suddenly blossomed into a real beauty. From then on she was rarely alone. The popular girls who had shunned Michelle in junior high felt betrayed. Now she was more popular than they were. Marla's claim to fame was appearing at school in a different outfit every day. She preferred expensive clothes guaranteed to make other girls jealous. Clothes were Marla's security blanket. Pam didn't like being a teenager. It seemed to her one long crisis after another. So she sneaked through the school corridors in drab clothes. She wasn't really mousy. Basically, Pam was very pretty. She just wasn't ready to let anyone know it.

Sound familiar? We'd be willing to bet that most teenage girls worry more about looks and popularity than about anything else. Competing for social position can become an obsession, particularly in junior high and the early high school years. Of course, the same could be said about boys. Who doesn't want to be sexy, attractive, and popular? For girls the problem is especially acute. Though women are in the work force in record numbers and girls have more opportunities to become lawyers, doctors, police officers, or whatever else they want, the idea that a girl should be "sugar and spice and everything nice" but not compete in a "man's world" hasn't vanished. Being pretty can still bring more praise than being smart. Many parents still consider a good marriage the main goal for their daughters. So it's hardly surprising that some girls consider beauty the only thing worth striving for and boyfriends the only measure of true success.

Dawn

Dawn's mother had encouraged her to be flirtatious and cute from the time she was in kindergarten. At eight she was given dancing lessons to make her graceful. At eleven she took a modeling course to learn how to put on makeup and style her hair. Dawn was a pretty girl who spent hours before the mirror trying to look sexy and sophisticated. By the time she reached high school all her efforts went into competing over boys.

Many teenage girls spend hours shampooing their hair, worrying about acne, exercising to lose weight, dieting to lose weight, buying clothes, sewing clothes, checking to see if their breasts are growing, if their bottom's too big, if their thighs are thick or thin. Teenagers are forever comparing themselves to an idealized image. As long as a girl maintains her grades, keeps playing the flute, softball, or even her stereo, and shows up promptly for her after-school job there's nothing to worry about. If all her energy goes into improving her looks and attracting boys, she's got a problem.

Dawn had to be the beauty of her group. She never made friends with anybody pretty. That way Dawn was sure to be the center of attention. She enjoyed bragging about her great love life and all the boys who thought she was terrific. She even promised to help her friends become more popular. In small ways she was helpful. Dawn had an eye for color and design and would help choose her friends' clothes, do their hair, and lend them jewelry. But whenever a girlfriend went on a diet, Dawn would tempt her with ice cream. If a boy liked one of Dawn's friends, Dawn would flirt with him. Boys and sex brought drama and excitement into Dawn's life. Never mind that all her friendships with girls ended in fights and tears.

Dawn never went out with any boy very long. Once a boy liked her, she became bored. It was time to move on, preferably to breaking up a solid couple. Next to making out, snatching away boys from other girls provided the highest drama of all. Unfortunately, equality was not the key word at Dawn's high school. Boys could get away with frequent sexual escapades. Girls who slept around were labeled sluts. Being labeled a slut didn't help Dawn make new girlfriends or get better treatment from teachers, who tended to write her off as a burnout anyway because her marks were low.

When Dawn was in a car accident, the rumor went around that Dawn had hurt her face and would need surgery. Ex-girlfriends gloated. It would "serve her right." Ex-boyfriends, most of whom had been publicly dumped by Dawn, didn't feel very sorry for her either. The rumor was false and Dawn emerged from the accident unscathed, but it wasn't easy returning to school and facing a total lack of sympathy. It wasn't easy learning a month later that no one cared whom she went to the prom with or wanted her at their table or would even share a limo with her on prom night. Though Dawn had been a source of gossip and interest in early high school, by junior year everybody was tired of her and nobody trusted her.

Like most compulsive competitors, Dawn was bound to lose. It was time for her to put the brakes on and think things through. Where had constant competitiveness brought her? Did she have girlfriends? No, merely satellites. Yet same-sex friendships are vital. Girls need girlfriends to confide in, to learn from, to share with, and to escape from the tensions of being with boys. Dawn saw every girl as a potential opponent to be trounced as thoroughly as if she were playing opposite her in a championship tennis match. Did Dawn have boyfriends? No, only conquests. She never gave herself enough time to find out what a boy was really like.

By summer, Dawn was determined to change. The opportunity came when she landed a summer job at a bakery. The only other person working with her behind the counter was a very pretty girl. Normally Dawn would have resented her. Now she made a conscious effort to be at least passingly friendly. Dawn found she actually liked the girl, but she wasn't ready to become friends with anybody quite so pretty yet.

Back at school Dawn tried out for a role in the senior play and got it. She discovered that she loved being in front of an audience and relished applause. Channeling her need for excitement and attention into the play gained her the respect of other students. They saw that she could be part of a cooperative effort and that she had talent.

Their respect made Dawn feel better about herself. People don't change instantly. Dawn still tried as hard as she could to steal the male lead away from his girlfriend. She would never be a candidate for the nicest-person-in-the-class award but she had made distinct progress. She was no longer an aggressive and self-destructive competitor in need of proving herself all the time.

ASSERTING ONESELF

Whereas Dawn spent hours a day on her appearance to attract boys and make girls jealous, clothes, looks, and style can be used competitively in more subtle ways for different purposes. After all, clothes, hair, and cosmetics make a statement. Dressing in the latest fashion shows the people around you that you are chic and sophisticated. Wearing ultra-advanced or simply oddball clothes stamps you as an individualist, an outcast, or a leader who can get away with being daring and ahead of the competition. Some girls dress quietly and conventionally. They prefer to merge with the crowd rather than stand out from their peers.

Some groups, fundamentalist Christians, for example, place great emphasis on appearance. Neatness, cleanliness, and wholesomeness are highly valued. Rebels generally go in for wild flamboyant styles including crazy haircuts, vivid hair dyes, or mad combinations of colors. This, too, is a form of asserting oneself, defining one's special place. Sometimes dressing in a radically different way from the people around you is a means of insulting and getting back at those you think rejected you. It isn't necessarily paranoid. Most high schools have at least one popular group considered ruthless and snobbish by those excluded from it. Of course, you never know. Something that looks weird today can catch on and be the ordinary style everybody conforms to tomorrow.

If it's any consolation, it's usually in the early teens that clothes, hair styles, and hair color are so enormously charged with meaning. By the mid- to late-teens people loosen up and become freer. But from junior high right through the first two years of high school the unwritten rules governing what you can wear safely are rigid. Every detail must be right. You don't roll up your sleeves if nobody you like, admire, respect, hate, or fear rolls up theirs. If everybody wears wide belts, lacy gloves, or shiny jackets, you wear them, too. Make a mistake and *wham!* Social disaster. You may as well wear a uniform for all the choice you have.

Relax, things will change. Meanwhile only you can decide how and to what extent you will use clothes competitively. If you feel comfortable playing it safe, don't worry about whether you're stuck with herd instinct. Just follow the crowd for now. You probably have enough on your mind as it is. You don't have to dress in a way that will make life tougher.

If, on the other hand, you want to flaunt the conventions, go ahead and dress differently. Just don't expect others to approve or rush out and copy you. Grown-ups complain a lot about the way kids dress. But there are worse ways to express what you feel and far more dangerous methods of getting attention than by adopting a look that sends the message you want to send to your peers.

Vicki

Some girls try to cope with the whole messy competitive business of boys, clothes, looks, and popularity by withdrawing from the process. Vicki had always been plump, but in eighth grade she became a compulsive eater. By the time she was fifteen, she was grossly overweight. Vicki had to face a whole constellation of problems at home and at school. Her parents fought constantly, and Vicki and her younger sister were intensely competitive. Though Vicki certainly didn't gain weight just to avoid competition around boys and sex, her weight kept her from competing. As far as Vicki was concerned, being overweight solved many problems.

Unlike Dawn, Vicki had no problem with attractive girls. She knew a lot of them. Her weight was a kind of badge announcing that Vicki was no threat to potential girlfriends. Boys liked Vicki, too. They didn't want to go out with her, but she was easy to be with. When a boy was near Vicki, there was no crackling tension. In a way Vicki had achieved a kind of lopsided popularity. She was every-body's friend, good old Vicki, the special case you could feel sorry for.

Vicki could ignore pressures that afflicted other girls. Vicki didn't go shopping for clothes very often. Vicki didn't wash her hair six times a week or get up an hour early in the morning to put on her makeup before school. She never concerned herself with getting a date for a dance because she knew perfectly well no one would go out with her. She could get to all the parties she wanted to go to and find someone to talk with. Her weight protected her like armor from the competitive fray that caused so many of her girlfriends so much suffering.

Actually what was happening to Vicki was disastrous, no escape at all. Like other girls, she dreamed of romance. Yet when she met a good-looking boy, she didn't dare let her interest show. She was afraid she'd be hurt, that she'd make a fool of herself. Feelings like this only made her eat more. She envied her girlfriends because they had dates, and sometimes she'd spread lies about them behind their backs. At night she would masturbate and cry herself to sleep.

When Vicki was a junior in high school, her family situation reached crisis proportions. Oddly enough it was probably just as well because at last the family sought out therapy. As Vicki began to cope more effectively with her parents, her sister, and her friends at school, she started losing weight.

Vicki could be charming and witty. She knew a lot about old movies and early rock 'n' roll. The inevitable happened. Once she'd slimmed down, boys found her attractive and interesting and asked her out. Vicki was terrified. Suddenly she had to contend with all the emotions and relationships that her obesity had kept in check. Fortunately, Vicki stuck to therapy instead of running away and getting fat again. It took a long time and it wasn't easy, but eventually Vicki learned to accept competition as an inevitable and even positive part of living.

Unlike Vicki most girls try their best to be pretty. They try so hard that sometimes to counteract what seems to be an obsession, girls are told that beauty isn't everything. By now you've probably heard the story about the class beauty regretting that she won the popularity contest. She knows she doesn't deserve it. Deep in her heart she wishes the class grind Velma Sue had won. Velma Sue has brains and talent. Poor class beauty is a vapid airhead with nothing to look forward to except a modeling career. Velma Sue will make a wonderful wife and mother someday, not to mention getting a law degree and being appointed to the state supreme court.

Chances are you can't work up much pity for the class beauty. Frankly, we can't either. If you were given your choice between being Velma Sue or being magically rivetingly gorgeous, which would you choose? We suspect you'd at least give the matter some thought. There's no getting away from it. Beauty is a distinct advantage. It gives you an edge with boys and contributes to general popularity. It is a relief (at least if you're not or don't consider yourself to be beautiful) to realize that beauty is not the only factor that counts. It doesn't automatically put you in the driver's seat on the road to Fantasyland. Consider Nancy. In her case being beautiful did mask problems.

Nancy

Blonde, pretty Nancy was basically shy. Because she'd always been a quiet merge-with-the-wallpaper type, she'd had few friends when she was little. After all, who cares if you're pretty in third grade? So Nancy was a loner whose closest companion was her very attractive mother. Nancy took dancing lessons with her mother. She put together a doll collection with her mother. She walked home from school every day with her mother.

Then Nancy turned twelve. Overnight, or so it seemed to Nancy, she grew tall and developed a slim sexy figure. While all about her others were sprouting zits, Nancy's complexion was peaches and cream. By thirteen Nancy was a source of interest to a number of individuals who had never noticed her before, mostly male. But whatever her appearance, Nancy was still Nancy inside—shy, scared, and very dependent on her mother.

Nancy's mother was proud of her own good looks and doubly proud of Nancy's. She'd always worried about Nancy's shyness and feared Nancy would be a lonely teenager. So when a popular tenth-grader named Ted asked

Nancy out when she was merely an eighth-grader, Nancy's mother encouraged her to say yes. Nancy knew she wasn't ready to go out with a boy in high school, but she wasn't strong enough to resist her mother. So she went out with Ted and, just as she'd feared, was plunged into an intense relationship too soon.

By high school Nancy was in the habit of relying on her looks. She was uncomfortable with girls and avoided them. She half wanted to join the photography club, the school newspaper, or the ski club, but she didn't dare. It was easier to cling to one steady boyfriend after another. She had no trouble finding guys. They found her. What's more, they rarely noticed how insecure she was, how lacking in any real self-confidence. Nancy looked great. She dressed well. That was all she needed or so it seemed.

When senior year rolled around, Nancy wasn't all that different from the shy girl she'd been in eighth grade. Four years of hiding in a cocoon hadn't allowed her to change, grow, reach out to new experiences, or mature. She was afraid of what life after graduation would hold, and getting married seemed the easiest way out. So she became engaged to a pleasant but rather bland boy who didn't know what to do with his life either. Unfortunately, Nancy was turning out much like her mother, who had also hidden behind her beauty rather than face up to her problems.

What would have happened if Nancy hadn't been beautiful? To be fair, she might have been isolated and miserable. But maybe in her misery she would have found a girlfriend and through her met other girls. Maybe along with her newfound friends she would have joined the ski club. That would have given her an interest and hobby. Perhaps a teacher, a guidance counselor, or even Nancy's mother would have recognized that she was unhappy.

Coming to this realization might have given Nancy's mother the strength to let go. If nothing else, at least Nancy would have been spared Ted, and that would have bought her time. But everyone just assumed that because Nancy was beautiful and popular with boys, she was okay. She wasn't.

PITFALLS FOR YOU AS MISS POPULARITY

Every girl lucky enough to be considered good-looking isn't awash in personal problems. What is there to say about competition to the girl who is beautiful and popular with girls as well as with boys, who is also a top student who exudes confidence, and who is in six extracurricular activities? Is there nothing to do but hand her the winner's crown?

Well, it's not quite that easy. There aren't many girls so blessed. But there are just enough so you probably know one. Maybe *you* are one. If so, let's take a look at the few pitfalls dotting the road to the Miss Popularity sweepstakes.

Everybody loves a high school superstar, right? No, wrong. Even people who like you and admire you are bound to feel some jealousy. It isn't easy watching someone else win all the elections and contests and receive all the awards. People just can't help but hope that somewhere somehow you'll take a big fall. They may even want to be there to push. The best way to undercut envy is to win graciously.

Try not to appear smug. Don't brag about your successes. Go out of your way to be nice to people who aren't members of your own clique. Don't downplay your attractiveness, but don't use your looks and popularity as a weapon to hurt other people's feelings or as a means of power. Remember, nobody's perfect. You have faults and weaknesses just as does everybody else, and though it may not seem like it now, you may need help and sympathy yourself someday. One thing's for sure. You don't need enemies hanging around waiting for the chance to be really nasty to you.

Tiffany

Tiffany was stunning. By junior year she was the most popular and sought after girl in her school. Academically she was third in her class. She was president of student council. Used to winning, she expected to win. That put her at a disadvantage when it came to losing. She had quite literally never learned how. So when it came time for the spring musical, Tiffany assumed she'd get the lead. She wanted the glory of stardom. She also enjoyed showing off her dazzling figure, and what better way than wearing a skimpy costume on stage in front of a large audience?

A couple of months before auditions for the spring musical there was a dance show at the high school, and Tiffany was given a solo. Tiffany came to rehearsals in gorgeous leotards and bodysuits. The other girls in the class resented the way Tiffany flaunted her beauty. Even the teacher grew a bit irritated with Tiffany's attitude. Tiffany seemed mainly interested in promoting Tiffany.

Tiffany performed her solo dance well. Her audition for the musical went well, too. But Tiffany didn't get the lead. Everyone from the teacher right through the students felt that Tiffany had had too much of the spotlight and that someone else should have a chance to excel.

The rejection came as a blow to Tiffany. Hurt, angry, and resentful, she was also shocked at the reaction of her so-called friends to her loss. For about a week after auditions people dropped little jabbing remarks her way, were rude and hostile, or offered phony expressions of sympathy.

Tiffany did wind up with a role in the show, and she did get to wear a skimpy costume. But she controlled her urge to show off and preen, and she learned to live with someone else's getting most of the applause. From now on she would be careful not to whip up envy because it would only mean trouble for her.

WINNING AND LOSING

Actually Tiffany was lucky to be able to grapple with this problem in high school. Just as learning to win graciously is important, you must be able to handle losing. The world is filled with high school superstars who are superstars no more after they graduate. For every prom queen who's the beauty of her class, there's another prom queen twice as pretty. You can't coast through life on your high school reputation.

Besides things change. Girls who aren't considered attractive in high school may seem very attractive later as they mature and develop a style of their own. Standards vary. Girls who seem gorgeous in high school may not be considered beauties later. Boys grow up, too, you know, and at least some of them will come to appreciate a pretty smile and vivacious charm more than a 38-D bra size.

Girls as well as boys tend to become more secure and confident once they're out of high school, freer to see past stereotypes. You may change your ideas about looks yourself. Guys you don't find attractive now may appeal to you when you get a little older. Try to bear this in mind and be polite when the class nerd asks you out.

Some teenage girls go off the deep end when it comes to looks, sex, and popularity. They are ready to do anything no matter how potentially dangerous just to look better.

It's not entirely their fault. Every time they turn on the television there's a commercial featuring a beautiful model. Every time they go to a film there's an actress so lovely they want to cry.

It's tough, but you really should try to resist the pressures to go to extremes just to look good. If you can't cope with this on your own consider getting help. Sometimes just talking to a sympathetic adult you trust will make it easier for you to keep your balance.

Sure it's great to look good in a bikini, but it isn't fatal if you don't. Lying under a sun lamp or on the beach all day to get a tan can prove fatal. Skin cancer is no joke. Watching your weight makes good sense, but don't take over-the-counter diet pills, and don't O.D. on diet sodas and celery stalks until you're weak and scrawny. Running to get in shape or stay in shape is fine. Exercise is good for you. But if you become a maniac as soon as you put on a pair of running shoes, slow down. Please don't rush into cosmetic surgery just because you don't like the shape of your nose or some other portion of your anatomy. There are risks in surgery, not least the risk of yielding to the phony value and superficial belief that only good looks can make your life change for the better. Wait awhile. This is one decision you can make when you're older. There are many over-the-counter medications for acne. Most don't work very well. If you have extreme acne, consult a dermatologist. There are effective methods of treatment, but they are potentially dangerous and you should weigh the risks carefully before you undertake them.

You can probably name several girls who aren't attractive but who are quite popular. That's because there's more than one way to achieve social position. So set some ground rules of your own when you compete. You might discover that you can be quite successful on your own terms.

•8•

"BE A MAN"

When Freddy entered high school he was five feet eleven and weighed 175 pounds. His solid frame had more muscle than baby fat. He was also very well coordinated. In the eyes of the coaches of Hamilton High, Freddy had football player written all over him. Freddy's dad had been a pretty fair lineman when he went to Hamilton. People in this football-mad community remembered that. "Like father, like son," they said. Freddy's dad dreamed that his son would "make him proud."

Freddy had played some football while still in junior high school, and he was pretty good at it, but he never really liked the game. In fact, he wasn't crazy about any competitive sports. Freddy liked music, and worse still—as far as the general opinion in his school was concerned—he liked classical music. Freddy kept his musical tastes to himself.

When he entered high school, Freddy tried out for junior varsity football—it was expected of him. He made the team with ease because of his size and he was a real addition. Though Freddy wasn't crazy about football, the game itself didn't really bother him. His problem was with the other players. He didn't like them; they didn't like him.

The regular season was bad enough, but the real horror for Freddy was football camp. Every summer the members of the team were sent to a two-week football camp—

all expenses paid by a couple of local fraternal organizations. Not only was it a free two weeks in the country, football camp was considered a great honor. As far as Freddy was concerned it meant that he was going to have to spend two weeks in close quarters with guys whom he hated. But it was an offer he couldn't refuse.

Football camp turned out to be every bit as bad as Freddy expected. As always, the game itself was fine. Indeed, a couple of coaches at the camp thought Freddy possessed real ability. After the practice, Freddy's life at camp was pure hell. Duke, one of the other team members, started calling Freddy "the fat faggot"—and that name went around the camp. Not only was Freddy tormented mercilessly, anybody who happened to get friendly with Freddy also became a victim. As a result very few wanted to be known as one of Freddy's friends.

One night somebody put frogs in Freddy's bed. On another he was doused with a pail of cold water in the middle of the night. Freddy was too big and too strong to be physically attacked—but he was severely hurt nonetheless. Worse yet, there was absolutely nothing he could do about it.

Freddy could have challenged Duke and fought him. But Freddy was no fighter, and he probably would have lost. Besides he was scared. Even if by some far-out chance Freddy had won a fight, the harassment wouldn't have stopped. Duke had friends at camp, Freddy didn't. He couldn't tell the counselors. They would have regarded such an action as "unmanly." "All you have to do is stand up to a bully," they would say. "Bullies are cowards. Stand up to them and they back down." They wouldn't understand that Duke was a bully but he wasn't a coward.

Freddy could have called his parents and asked to go home early. His father wouldn't have understood either and probably would have been angry and hurt that his son would behave like such a wimp. So Freddy stuck it out for two of the most miserable weeks of his life.

When he got back to school Freddy found that the mere prospect of going to football practice made him feel sick. He became depressed, and his schoolwork suffered. Problems multiplied until his parents were forced to take him out of the public school and put him into a small private school, without a football team. It was a move the family really could not afford, but they could see no other option.

Away from the pressures of having to be a high school jock, Freddy was much happier, and his schoolwork once again improved.

Poor Freddy. He had been trapped, forced to compete in an area in which he really didn't belong. It's not that he was physically incapable of playing football—quite the contrary. His life might have been considerably easier if he had been small. No one would have pressured him. It was that he couldn't compete in the world of the high school jock.

COMPETITION ON THE PLAYING FIELD

No matter what the rhetoric about a new emphasis on academic achievement and about encouraging the development of a wide range of abilities and talents, in many high schools, probably most high schools in the United States, athletics is what is considered most important for boys. Parents, particularly fathers, want to see their sons compete on the playing field. In addition to the pure pleasure of wishing to see one's child compete successfully in something, athletics also gives fathers a reassuring confirmation of their son's "manliness." Because he plays football, he must be all right!

In many schools coaches are under very real pressures to put together a winning team. Any likely looking prospect is going to be encouraged to play, whether he really wants to or not.

For the successful high school athlete the rewards are obvious and immediate. For the student who succeeds in academics or the arts the payoff is usually slower and less obvious.

In most of our lives athletic activity peaks in high school. There is no time in your life when sports will be more important. It's great to be a successful high school athlete. You don't need to be told that.

For the rest, those of you who didn't make the team or didn't even try—be patient. Once high school is over, you will never have to face the heavy pressure to compete athletically again. Just hang in there. Try not to become so discouraged and angry that you find yourself avoiding all forms of sports and physical activity. A friendly, noncompetitive game of softball or tennis can be lots of fun, even if you're not very good at the game. Running, bike riding, and swimming are all good for you, even if you don't set any school records. If you're not competitive athletically, try to keep the sports in perspective. Relax and enjoy the activity for its own sake.

SEXUAL COMPETITION

Next to sports the area in which competition among teenage boys is fiercest though much less public is sex.

Over the last fifteen years or so there has been a good deal of talk about a revolution in attitudes toward sex. It's been said that the double standard, which holds that what's forbidden to girls is not only accepted but desirable for boys, is dead. Attitudes probably have softened somewhat, but the double standard is still alive and reasonably well in most American high schools. Just look around you. A girl who has the reputation for sleeping with lots of guys is known as "easy" or even "a slut." While virginity *per se* isn't held in particularly high esteem anymore, few girls will compete openly over the number and speed of their sexual conquests. When they do, it's often an uncomfortable and defiant pose.

It's quite different for boys. The guy who has the reputation of having sex with lots of girls is macho—a real man. Even if he has the reputation of being something of a louse, it's still an epithet tinged with respect and envy. Many parents accept the double standard at least unconsciously. In fact, if a teenage boy isn't sexually active, some parents begin to worry.

Sports are public. Your accomplishments or lack of them are right out there for everyone to see. Sex is an activity that is generally performed in private, so it's difficult to check up on who's doing what. If a guy and a girl go out together, you have no real way of knowing whether they spent the night holding hands and watching television or if they checked into the "Fantasy Island Motel—Rooms By the Hour." If a friend tells you that he's been sleeping with Mrs. Jones while her husband is away on business trips, you may chose to believe him or not—but you probably have no way of actually knowing.

The situation is this: There is great pressure on teenage boys to be very sexually active, but no one can prove anything. As a result there is a great deal of exaggeration and downright lying going on.

When a group of boys sits around to talk about sex, the usual practice is to try to top one another with accounts of sexual activity. Anyone who is rather inexperienced or—heaven forbid—a seventeen-year-old virgin—is going to feel very left out indeed. So he's probably going to lie. Not to worry; the other guys are lying too.

Sexual competition among teenage boys has some very unfortunate side effects. The guy who is building his own reputation, bragging about how he had this or that girl the other night, may also be tearing down the reputation of the girls.

Sexual competition can also become a numbers game—in which the connection between sex and affection is lost. If the aim is simply to score with as many girls as possible, then it really isn't important whether you like or respect the girl. Indeed, the easier the conquest, the more likely a boy is to feel contempt.

There is another unhappy side effect to sexual competition: it puts teenage boys under great pressure to perform. Many boys feel that they have to perform and perform well sexually the first time and every time. With all the other guys bragging about what great lovers they are, you may feel you can't keep up, that you are a failure, perhaps not "normal." These kinds of anxieties can create problems, which in turn increase the anxieties, which intensify the problems, and so on. It's a vicious circle.

The best advice is relax—you're not superman, and you don't have to be. The guy who tells you that he is is a liar. If you're really worried, you might want to talk to a doctor if you can find one who is sympathetic and easy to talk to. There are counselors and therapists and about a million books on sex that you can read. In this case, talking to your friends and getting their advice is probably not such a hot idea. They have as much misinformation as you do.

In our society sex is a highly charged, complex, and very delicate subject. It involves a lot more than simple physical gratification. To make sex another area of competition in which you must "win," in which you must prove yourself, distorts and dehumanizes sex. When that happens, you become a real loser.

DANGEROUS COMPETITION

Teenage boys often compete in activities involving danger and physical abuse.

Dominick was a chubby, robust boy. At the age of twelve and thirteen he would sometimes show off by drinking a dozen root beers in a row. It was a silly thing to do, and he usually felt pretty sick afterward, but his friends were impressed. It was his way of showing off—of being special. By the time he was sixteen, Dom turned to real beer. He could down a whole bottle without taking a breath, drink a six-pack at a single sitting. He challenged anyone in the room to match him drink for drink—no one could. Of course, he got terribly drunk and suffered monumental hangovers, but for a while that didn't seem to matter. He could drink more than anyone else in his crowd—and he was proud of that. It gave him status.

Many teenage boys go through that sort of phase; fortunately most get over it. Dom did. His friends finally got tired of watching good old Dom pass out at parties. Dom got tired of waking up on Sunday mornings wishing he were dead. He still drank at parties, but he no longer felt he had to drink more than everyone else. He discovered that he didn't have to be a clown in order to have people notice him. If someone else wanted to be the first to pass out—let him. Dom had retired from that competition.

Dom was lucky. Drinking yourself into oblivion can be dangerous. People have died from bouts of heavy drinking. Though he had often fallen down, Dom had never seriously injured himself, and he didn't know how to drive. But drunken driving and other alcohol-induced accidents are a leading cause of death among teens—possibly the leading cause. Being the biggest beer-guzzling goof in your crowd is just plain stupid.

Teenage boys have lots of other ways of trying to demonstrate who's the toughest, the strongest, the most daring. In some areas it's fighting, illegal drag racing, or other highly risky activities. In one form or another this sort of activity occurs in many societies. The young warrior has to prove himself physically before being fully accepted as a man by the tribe.

Displays of blind courage might be useful if you lived at a time when you had to fight off grizzly bears. But you don't live in a primitive society. You're probably not going to face a lot of physical dangers, except those that you make for yourself. Risking your neck just for the sake of risking your neck isn't brave—it's dumb.

•9•
CLIQUES AND CLUBS

There are very few popular loners. In high school a person's popularity rating often depends on which clique he or she belongs to. Theresa, Joan, and Cathy had wanted to be football cheerleaders from the time they joined Pop Warner cheerleaders in sixth grade. Football cheerleaders were the girls' high school superstars. The trio of Joan, Theresa, and Cathy would sit in the stands at home games watching their ideal versions of human perfection kick, shout, smile, and form pyramids.

The three girls worked very hard, and by the end of eighth grade they were ready for junior varsity tryouts. Their archenemy was Deborah, who had scored the highest among the Pop Warner cheerleaders and who had never liked them. The feeling was mutual. Facing such stiff competition, Cathy, Theresa, and Joan practiced together. Each admired the others and urged them on, yet each tried to be the best of the three. They knew that 90 percent of the girls who tried out for cheerleading wouldn't make it.

Although the girls were close, they weren't triplets, and each evolved a different routine. Theresa was tall and mature, so she did a formal routine. Cathy was short and cute, and so she worked up a peppy routine. Joan had studied gymnastics and was the best acrobat of the group. However, there was no way to prepare completely for the brutal competition of the tryout itself. Joan dreamed of murdering Deborah, and Cathy even dreamed about murdering Joan.

When Theresa's turn came, her heart pounded, her mouth was dry, and she felt wobbly. After the tryouts, Cathy was coldly calm and confident, but Joan tried to forget the whole experience. When the names of the girls who had made cheerleaders was posted, Theresa was the only one who had the courage to go read the list.

Tryouts are tricky, and Theresa was delighted and surprised to see that Deborah hadn't made cheerleaders. It was a stunning upset, and Deborah never tried out for cheerleaders again. Theresa was overjoyed to see her own name on the list and Cathy's. Poor Joan hadn't made it. But Joan wasn't easily discouraged, and next year she tried again and this time she succeeded. Still, she had to spend her whole freshman year watching Cathy and Theresa being smugly superior. It galled knowing they felt sorry for her. Though she remained their friend, things weren't the same. They were cheerleaders and therefore popular. She couldn't attend practices or dress like a cheerleader, so though she was a member of the right clique, she was definitely at the bottom of the pecking order.

Sophomore year was different. Now Joan, too, got to lead pep rallies, date one of the boys on the football team, and walk around the school as if she owned it. Naturally, things didn't run smoothly. Though Theresa's mother had been a cheerleading coach and so was proud of her daughter, and Cathy's mother had been a varsity cheerleader and came to all the games, Joan's mother had never been a cheerleader. She kept harping about how Joan's grades would suffer if she spent so much time cheering and suggested Joan try something less involving like field hockey instead.

Many people at school resented cheerleaders. The worst offenders were girls who had tried out and hadn't made it themselves and who now pretended they'd never really wanted to be cheerleaders in the first place. They called Cathy, Theresa, and Joan snobs and fluffy-headed dummies. True, the three girls weren't the top students in the school, but at least one of the varsity cheerleaders was second in her class and nobody was flunking. Yes, they did spend a lot of time putting on makeup and making sure they looked good, but appearance is an important part of cheerleading and that didn't make them fools. What was especially irritating was getting cold treatment from kids who used to be their friends but who now resented their popularity.

In a way, though, provoking all the envy and rudeness was part of the fun of being a cheerleader. Joan, Theresa, and Cathy liked being members of an identifiable group. It wasn't really anything about them as individuals that made them popular, it was being a cheerleader. None of the three was glamorous or scintillating or fascinating. If they hadn't been cheerleaders, they would have been indistinguishable from most of the girls in their class.

Still, even with all the pluses, which they wouldn't have traded for the world, there was a hollow side to their glory. It wasn't glorious enough. To outsiders they looked as if they had everything and that everything came easily. Actually Joan, Theresa, and Cathy felt they were underappreciated. Nobody seemed to realize how much hard work went into cheerleading and how demanding it was. The image of cheerleaders as silly girls who were just an adjunct to the boys' team was false and painful to live with. Cheerleading was really a form of athletics in its own right, complete with its own formal competitions. When you cheered, your attitude had to be just right; your ability to work in unison was critical. You had to smile even when you sweated. It wasn't easy leading pep rallies, trying to whip up the crowd and get them roaring while the school brains sat and stared at you sullenly and a lot of girls refused to applaud your routines.

You had to stand by and watch the football players get all the credit. Unless the cheerleaders won a major competition and got to Florida and were on television, the school didn't care whether they won their competitions or not. The jocks had the prestige. Though it was the cheerleaders' job to decorate the lockers of the boys on the football team before games and give them candy and encourage them, the boys just teased them or brushed them aside. Sometimes Theresa, Joan, and Cathy half hoped their team would lose. Who cared as long as the cheering went well?

Then there was the time the girls' basketball team was second in the league, and though it was embarrassing, the cheerleaders went out and cheered for the girls' basketball team. At least the girls' team appreciated the gesture, and it did help raise the pride and spirit of the team, which usually got no recognition at all.

The time involved, two hours of practice five days a week, caused lots of problems. If they so much as failed a quiz, teachers blamed the failure on their cheering. Many teachers couldn't stand cheerleaders anyway and went out of their way to make an example of them whenever they did anything wrong. Other people could get away with things. Cheerleaders never could. One slip and you were in trouble.

But Joan, Theresa, and Cathy tried not to worry about the things they didn't like about cheerleading. They got to go to cheerleading camp together during the summer, and that was great. They went to the same parties, and the best parties in the school were held after the games. These were the parties of the football players and the cheerleaders. Other people came, but the members of the team and the cheerleaders were the center of attention, and when the team won, the parties were super. At times like these when there were outsiders around, Cathy, Joan, and Theresa and the other cheerleaders behaved as a unit. It was one for all and all for one. Alone, when the cheerleaders were among themselves, it was different.

Close as they were, Theresa was always cutting up Joan, and Joan fought like crazy with Cathy, who was always out to get Theresa, who could be really vicious to Cathy. But they banded together when it came to the rest of the cheerleaders. Some of the other cheerleaders were their friends and they liked them. Some they hated, especially Ann who flirted with the boys on the opposing team and their very own captain who bossed them mercilessly. Then there were the senior cheerleaders who were horrible. They felt like breaking into a cheer when two seniors were replaced by juniors at that year's tryouts.

Still, the cheerleaders were really there for each other when it counted, putting their personal squabbles aside. In their junior year the mother of one of the cheerleaders died, and the whole group reached out to the girl. They invited her to sleep over. They were patient during practices. If it hadn't been for the help of the other cheerleaders, the girl might have fallen apart. It was so important to have a really strong group on your side in high school.

THE IMPORTANCE OF GROUPS

This is probably the most clique- or group-centered time of your life. As people grow older, they tend to have fewer friends, preferring a small circle of close acquaintances to a crowd. Often they cherish their privacy. Teens are usually just the opposite. Though everybody wants to be alone occasionally, by and large adolescents crave company. They drive around in groups. They go to movies in groups. They cluster together in cliques in the school cafeteria. Hanging out with others is a favorite pastime, and when they come home, the first thing teenagers do is grab the phone to talk to the same people they've just seen. Behavior like this often drives parents wild, but it is important and positive. Later you'll strike out more on your own. Right now you need the protection of being part of a group. Besides, groups are exciting and dynamic, filled with the kind of intrigue that makes life interesting.

Cliques have their good points. They promote cooperation and provide a support that is nonexistent when you compete one-on-one. You strive together with others, even though you strive against rival groups. Of course, there is competition within groups. Cathy, Theresa, and Joan were always trying to push ahead of each other and climb another rung higher on the social ladder. But, basically, they were buoyed up by the cheerleading group and one another.

If you are on the outside looking in, it's comforting to know that members of cliques aren't as secure as they seem or as solidly sure of themselves as they like to appear. Somebody's always trying to dethrone the leader of a group from within. Somebody's always trying to push somebody else out of the clique and get in or move up in the group's esteem. So even though a clique presents the image of being tight, tough, and together, it's more show than reality.

Despite the pushing, shoving, and clawing within a group, it provides relief. You can withdraw into any clique and hide, and everybody needs to hide sometimes. You may be able to achieve leadership within a clique when you can't in the wider world of the entire class or school. Setting the pace for a small group is much easier than trying to set it for everybody. When you're part of a clique, you have a ready-made group of friends. You may not like them all, but then again not everybody will like you.

Nevertheless, you have a place. You're not alone.

Cliques allow ordinary people a chance to shine. Theresa, Joan, and Cathy weren't beautiful or charismatic, yet they became high school superstars because they were in a superstar group. In contrast, people who might otherwise find themselves isolated can often achieve social position by joining extracurricular activities that encourage a wide membership. They may not be members of a select group like the cheerleaders, but as a member of band, yearbook staff, SADD, Key Club, or the school newspaper they can find a sense of belonging. School organizations always need somebody willing to serve the group and keep it running.

People who compete too hard on an individual level have a lot to gain from joining an after-school club, provided they don't instantly try to dominate everyone in sight. The girl who can't see anything but beauty as a route to popularity might be pleasantly surprised to discover that joining the photography club and putting time and energy into it can do more to enhance her social status than ladling on the mascara. Shy kids, say the boy who likes computers and hates sports, can raise their social ante by joining the AV club, the math team, or any after-school club that will bring them into contact with people who share a similar interest.

Cliques definitely have their ugly side. Cliques, fraternities, sororities, and such can be brutally snobbish. They can close their members off from others and reinforce narrow values. People who aren't in popular cliques often feel hurt and rejected. So if you can possibly help it, try to move beyond your particular group from time to time. That applies both to those who are zipping along oozing social status and to those who consider themselves first-rank nerds. If you can't move beyond your own particular group of friends in school, then try when you're away from school. There are community centers, Y's, church groups, colleges offering special Saturday programs for high school students, dance classes, art courses at museums, pools, gyms, lots of places to join and meet new people. It's a big wide world out there with lots of different kinds of people. Get to know a few.

Like anything else, the search for popularity shouldn't become all-consuming. Don't join an extracurricular activity just because you want acceptance. It helps to have at least a glimmer of interest in the activity itself even if it's bare minimum curiosity as to whether it's something you'd enjoy. Remember, if you don't work and contribute to the group, you will not be looked upon as an asset, merely as a hanger-on. That won't win you friends.

Making it into a clique can bring its own share of problems. Have your marks dropped because you're busy socializing? Within limits that's okay. Few students can earn "A's" all the time, and the social side of life is important. If you're in the midst of a personal crisis or about to play the game of the season or if you're star of the high school play, your marks may dip. As long as the dip is temporary and not too extreme, it's not panic time. However, if you're partying so hard your marks are plunging, you've got a problem. If you're spending all your time with people you don't like or who treat you with contempt just because they're members of a popular clique, you've got a problem.

You're competing the wrong way. Sooner or later botching academics will catch up with you. Those people you're currying favor with, do they really accept you as a full-fledged member of their group or are you a satellite? If they bore you or you bore them, ask yourself if you wouldn't be happier with other people. So what if they're less popular. They'd be friends.

You also have to ask yourself how far you're willing to go to find approval within a clique. By their very nature cliques make for strong peer pressure. If the members of your clique get drunk three nights a week, smoke two packs of cigarettes a day, and skip school four days a week, it's pretty tough to say no to such antics—even if you want to. In some cliques drugs are the thing. The enormous dangers are either minimized or actually become part of the attraction. It's the "forbidden fruit" syndrome. Some cliques pride themselves on being outlaws, bold, defiant, and adventurous. When these kinds of cliques become violent, they're gangs. Now we're not suggesting you walk around with a halo or have "Saint" stamped across your forehead. You certainly don't have to admire that teenage ideal of adults Miss Goody Two-Shoes civics class president or Mr. Wonderful, who polishes apples for the Latin teacher. But for your own safety and well-being we urge you to use your best judgment when joining a group.

If you are not comfortable with the group's behavior as a whole or if you feel deep down that it's destructive, quit. We know that's easier said than done. You may be on your own and lonely for a while. You may find you're a member of a group that doesn't want to let go. You may have to seek outside help to break away. But it's better than hanging around with a crowd that's wrong for you.

LEGENDS OF THE SCHOOL

Jared, Kent, and Craig were the legends of their high school. When Michael met them, they were juniors and he was a freshman, so he felt enormously flattered when they let him hang around the fringes of their clique. They seemed to have everything going for them. They were bold and adventurous, able to get just about any girl they liked. They had lots of money and owned spectacular cars. And they were notorious for breaking the rules.

Jared was probably the smartest person in high school, and he was coolly proud that despite this he was barely earning "C's." Kent, a talented athlete, had been kicked off the football team. Craig, the most forceful, was the leader of the group. He was the one who usually thought up their most lavish pranks.

To Michael, who wasn't very adventurous, who had to work every Saturday at his father's deli, and who had never had a girlfriend, making friends with the titanic trio was like something out of a movie. They knew all the exciting places in town. Through them he met a lot of older and very interesting people. When the guys drove around, they picked up girls. Once they even picked one up for him. The girls sat on the guys' laps as the car went speeding and screeching through the streets. Michael was terrified that the cops would stop them, but luckily they managed to reach the park without being stopped. There they guzzled beer and pawed the girls, all except Michael who felt incredibly clumsy and appallingly stupid. Jared made so much fun of him for his shyness that the next time they took a drive together Michael picked up a girl from school he didn't particularly like and did his desperate best to seduce her.

He was not allowed to join his friends on their more flamboyant excursions, however. There was the night the three boys "borrowed" a hearse from a funeral home and left it parked in front of the principal's house with a coffin inside. They bragged about the incident at school and clowned around about it, but they were never officially caught. Then there was the time the trio went careening around the country club at night in some of the club's golf carts and destroyed them. Their parents paid for the damage, and the boys got away with the stunt. On occasion the clique could get very rough. Kent would go around bashing kids he didn't like, while Jared amused himself smashing cars with baseball bats.

Although being with them was so exhilarating that it lifted Michael right out of the monotony of ordinary life, which seemed to consist mainly of science tests these days, he was scared. What if he happened to be with the guys when they pulled off something really dangerous? What if Craig, Jared, or Kent got caught? Worse yet, what if Michael got caught? He could imagine his parents' reaction. What would his teachers say? Of course, he would be something of a hero among his peers, but what price heroism?

Summer came as a positive relief. Michael was busy working. Then he went on vacation with his family. That left little time for hanging around with the guys. Once he ran into Craig, who told him he had found out where to buy cocaine and offered to take Michael with him sometime to get it. He spent an evening getting drunk with Kent who was wearing a school football jersey covered with obscenities about the team, which he planned to present to the quarterback at the homecoming game next year. But for the most part Michael went his own way that summer and Craig, Jared, and Kent went theirs.

In the fall Jared was a junior again, having at last succeeded in flunking two courses, so Michael was only a year behind him in school. Michael sensed the clique was willing to include him more often in fun and games. He had no idea why except that maybe they needed an audience, somebody around they could always impress. Certainly he wasn't equal to them. The most he could hope for was a kind of nervous bravado.

He went to a few parties with the guys. That gave him status. But he didn't like being with them once he got there. They were too frenzied. He liked to listen to tapes quietly, and they just wanted to get drunk and take off for the next party. Actually, Michael was beginning to grow bored with them. Now that he was a sophomore, school was better. He was more involved in it and had made some new friends. He had a new interest, too, bodybuilding. Every day now he worked out in a gym. Though Kent, strong as he was, could have developed an incredibly muscular body, he didn't have the discipline to work out. The clique couldn't stick to anything for very long.

So by Christmas, Michael was seeing a lot less of the legendary Craig, Kent, and Jared. Not that he was mad at them. Actually, he was grateful to them. Thanks to the guys he'd had some terrific adventures that got even better when he told them to his more innocent friends. The guys had helped him grow up by introducing him to many older interesting people, and despite the "macho stuff," they'd helped him become more confident around girls. He knew where the exciting clubs and bars in town were, even though he was too young to get into any of them without Craig who could talk his way into just about any place.

But all and all he'd just as soon not risk any further adventures with the guys. He had no desire to go around beating people up or wrecking cars, and he might be expected to do precisely that if he remained friends with them long enough. Besides, what if they turned their violence on him? Part of the reason they were so charismatic was just because they were unpredictable and potentially dangerous. You never knew what they might do next. Michael knew that the next thing he would do would be to start running with a different crowd.

•10•
PLAYING YOUR OWN GAME

Some teenagers can't or won't compete. They daydream when they should be concentrating on their studies. They skip homework assignments and cut classes. They don't try out for teams. Socially they are nowhere, mere numbers in anonymous big schools, on the outs even in small schools. They keep falling farther and farther back, until catching up seems almost impossible. Other kids call them burnouts. Guidance counselors refer to them as low achievers. It seems as if they are only spectators watching others race to success. This is unfair.

LEARNING TO COMPETE

The person who can't compete may be very intelligent and highly talented but if he or she is miserably unhappy at home, has a physical problem, or has been put under excessive pressure to succeed he or she may just collapse and withdraw from challenges. If running away has become your pattern in dealing with life, it's time to consider getting help. Fantasies may provide a solid escape valve, but they're no substitute for recognition in the real world. As for making friends, well, no relationship is completely free of competitive elements. If you want friends, you'll have to compete for and with them, but the support you get from a relationship makes the competing worth while. You haven't really given up trying to compete or you wouldn't be reading this book. Keep in mind that everybody has special abilities. You do, too. You'll find life easier and happier once you start living up to your potential. So start talking to an adult you trust, be it a guidance counselor, a member of the clergy, a family member you feel comfortable with, a therapist. Maybe you need someone to help you find the right therapist. Perhaps you need to be part of a group of teenagers who are working to solve their problems. If you don't know where else to turn, begin by phoning a teen hot line. Don't wait. We hope you'll start now so things can get better soon.

By and large most people are up to some level of competing. They may not choose the usual areas: sports, popularity, or academics. But even though they run against the crowd or to the side of it, that doesn't make them uncompetitive nor does it make them losers.

Seth

Seth, fifteen, moved from a small town to a big city. His new high school was overwhelming, a tough place even for aggressive kids to make a splash. It was the first time Seth had ever encountered racial tensions and a high dropout rate or taken public transportation instead of a school bus to school. Everybody was already locked into groups and the cliques were tight. Nobody was looking for new recruits. Seth had played baseball and soccer in his hometown, but those sports didn't count for much at this city school. The only popular sport was basketball, but some very competitive and talented black kids dreaming about the NBA had a lock on that, putting it definitely out of Seth's five-feet-eight reach.

For months Seth wandered within his new high school, isolated, lonely, and so down he wanted to run away from home and hitchhike back to the place he'd come from. But Seth was realistic enough to know that wasn't possible. Since sports weren't working for him, Seth tried talking to people in his classes, just a friendly word or two. But they were either cold and distant or they were verbally competitive, and all he got for being nice was a lot of abuse in the form of city wit and sharp wisecracks. Seth felt outclassed again. Although he thought about girls all the time, he was too shy to approach any, and since he wasn't particularly good-looking, they didn't flock to him in the halls or hang around his locker.

Seth's one abiding interest was rock music, especially heavy metal. So Seth took advantage of living in a city and started going to lots of rock concerts. He had to admit that was one thing he hadn't been able to do in his faraway little town. At one of the concerts he spotted a kid from his school, and they started talking about music. It turned out that the other kid played the guitar. Seth wasn't a musician, but that didn't matter because Seth made a great audience. Soon he was over at his newfound friend's house all the time listening to records. One thing led to another, and within a few months Seth had a whole network of acquaintances who were rock fans and enough friends to form a small cohesive group at his school. He no longer had to walk down the halls alone or eat lunch in the cafeteria by himself.

When Seth turned sixteen, he got a part-time job and spent most of his money on tapes, discs, and records. Soon he had quite a collection. By now he knew not only fans but musicians and corresponded regularly with a California-based heavy metal band with a coterie of devoted followers. His in with the band gave Seth enormous prestige at school, especially with people who really knew their music. Seth became the school's heavy metal expert, and all kinds of kids came up to him when they had a question about music. He was to music what the kid who knows all about baseball stats is to baseball. Whenever anybody challenged Seth's facts or opinions, he argued his case forcefully, which surprised nobody more than Seth. He got the reputation of being a bit weird but very smart in his own way, somebody to reckon with.

Seth knew he had arrived when the editor of the school paper asked him to write reviews of rock concerts. Seth discovered he liked to write. He had never contemplated the future, but it occurred to him that he ought to go to college after he graduated high school and study communications, maybe become a rock critic or even a D.J., an idea that would once have terrified him. Okay, so they were dream ambitions, but so what? They were far from impossible dreams. Seth was now sure of himself. He recognized his own abilities, and in his own field of interest he could stand up to anybody. By competing outside the mainstream he had found a place for himself accomplishing a lot more than he would have had he futilely run for class president or wasted time knocking himself out trying to get on the basketball team.

OBSTACLES TO COMPETING

Some people have trouble competing because they're really shy, and some people can't handle competition because they're afraid of failure. They haven't yet learned the valuable lesson that failing at something doesn't make you a failure as a human being. Then there are people who can't compete easily because they're afraid of success. They believe they don't really deserve to win, that if they do, it's a mistake and they're a fraud.

Let's tackle some of these obstacles to competing successfully. Do you set reasonable goals? If like Seth you have a glimmering of where you'd like life to take you and you dream big, that's fine. The shy boy often imagines himself surrounded by gorgeous girls or pictures himself whisking the most popular girl in the school off for a weekend. The shy girl who doesn't go out often daydreams that movie stars are beating down her door. By the way, shy people don't have a monopoly on these particular fantasies. The most outgoing kids in the class have them, even that notorious exhibitionist and cynic, the class clown. He too may dream of being the romantic hero.

But daydreams are one thing and crazy goals are another. Crazy goals are self-defeating. If you're shy and you give yourself ten days to become the biggest extrovert in the school, you're setting yourself up to fail. If you decide you must become a straight "A" student when you're a "C-" student and nothing less will do, you're inviting failure. Maybe you can become an "A" student in time if you work hard enough. Maybe you can't. Either way, setting a lofty unattainable goal is a mistake and in the end a cop-out.

Set a tangible goal, and give yourself enough time to achieve it. Begin with small steps. If you're afraid of competition, trying to psyche yourself up by rushing madly into something only makes matters worse. You'll wind up where you started, and you'll hate yourself for it. Build your confidence, don't tear it down. It might help to remind yourself that one of the best reasons for competing with others is not to prove yourself but simply to find out what your own talents and interests really are. It's hard to find out when you're hiding.

If you believe that quaking at the very thought of competition makes you a poor competitor, think again. What's so great about the superaggressive "must win 'em all" type who can't even play a game of tennis without being scared he or she will lose? One reason this aggressive type wins trophies is because he or she doesn't dare *not* win trophies. Sometimes you should play tennis or any other game because it's fun. So at least you just have to contend with being a timid competitor; the compulsive competitor never savors the success he or she earns. For the compulsive competitor winning merely sets the stage for climbing the ladder to the next and tougher level of competition—with no end in sight.

To make it easy on yourself, start by competing with yourself. What do you enjoy? Some people are movie buffs. Others read romances by the crateful. Some teenagers collect comic books. Maybe you'd like to play the piano. Choose something very private, very much your own, and like Seth, work your way up to becoming something of an expert. When you work toward your goals in private, nobody can make you uncomfortable or make fun of you. You're free to make mistakes unobserved. When you feel ready, when you have the knowledge or the skill, then you can go public. You may not even have to. For instance, who's to know that you have set a goal for yourself of getting a mark of "C" on an English paper after getting "D's" all semester? If you don't get the "C" the first time around, keep trying. When you get the "C" or you find the elusive early Marvel comic that will be a great addition to your collection or you've tracked down a tape of that old Humphrey Bogart film you've been searching for, then treat yourself. Have an ice cream. Buy yourself a sweater. Do something nice for yourself. You deserve it.

Try to meet people who share your interest. Then you'll

have something to talk about. You don't have to find friends only at your school. Check out fan clubs, go to sci fi conventions. If you've got a sneaking desire to excel at sports, start with running. You can run alone. Any sport where you compete with yourself against your own past performance is easier to take than team sports, which involve direct competition with others, often in front of an audience. Karate helps some people build confidence. So does bodybuilding. You can paint alone in your room and you can write poetry by yourself. If you want to show someone your creations, you can target a person you like and trust.

When you do decide to share your interest, be it photography or video, or you decide to exhibit a painting in the school's art show, you may be pleasantly surprised to discover that your efforts are appreciated. Take pride in what you do. You don't have to be the best to enjoy a project for its own sake. The important thing is not the prize, it's how you feel.

Janis

Janis had always dreamed of being a serious artist. She worked hard at her goal. Even in elementary school she was forever drawing her pet cat, her mother's portrait, her best friend's house. Along the way her teachers encouraged her, none more than her high school art teacher Mrs. Udell. But Janis was a perfectionist and very sensitive. She hated criticism, interpreting anything short of total admiration as an attack. She would be the world's greatest painter or at least one of the greatest painters of the century. Nothing less would do. Janis often imagined herself showing her works at a famous museum while patrons lined up at her studio door to buy paintings. She was quick to destroy paintings she had worked on diligently if they fell below her standard.

Janis wasn't generally competitive outside of art. She was content to get "B's" in her classes. She couldn't have told you the name of the quarterback of the school football team. However, she was deeply in love and eager to get the attention of a very attractive and popular boy named James, who was in her French class. When Janis wasn't thinking about painting, she was thinking about him. Basically shy, she had no idea how to get to know James.

Mrs. Udell came to her rescue. She suggested that Janis practice conversations on a tape. At first the suggestion struck Janis as hopelessly stupid and embarrassing, but she was desperate enough to give it a try. Pretending that she was talking to James, she tried different gambits, different ploys, and responded to his imaginary questions and answers. She even tried role-playing in front of her mirror. Since nobody could see her or hear her, she didn't have to worry about making a fool of herself.

Janis's art teacher also urged her to enter a portfolio in the state summer school of the arts competition. If she was accepted, she would spend a month on a college campus along with other talented high school students. Janis slaved over her portfolio, becoming so tense she had trouble painting anything at all. At last when the deadline was staring her in the face, she submitted the portfolio. A month passed and then she got the word. It was no. Her portfolio was returned to her. Janis cried for hours. Her teacher tried to console her, but it was no use. Janis wasn't just disappointed or even heartbroken. She was crushed. Mrs. Udell pointed out that Janis could try again the following summer, that she shouldn't give up. She was very talented. If the judges at the summer school of the arts couldn't see this, other judges would recognize her gifts someday. She had a future. Tactfully, Mrs. Udell hinted that setting the goal of being the greatest painter of the century was fine in the abstract but rigid and unrealistic in the here and now. Even if Janis never became a fine artist, she could always find satisfying work as a designer or illustrator.

But Janis was too defeated to hear. If she couldn't be the best, she wouldn't paint. That was that. Luckily, things worked out well with James. After three attempts Janis finally got up the nerve to squeak out a few words to him. His reply wasn't exactly what she'd anticipated from her conversations with his imaginary counterpart on tape and her own answer wasn't smooth, but it was a start. By the end of the week she was easily talking with James, and by summer they were going out. Mrs. Udell was happy that Janis had coped so well with James but very sorry that she had given up painting. She could only hope that Janis would continue painting someday because she had a genuine contribution to make.

EXTREME SHYNESS

Then there's the really shy person.

Does your throat turn dry, your hands shake, your face get red when people look at you? Oh, sometimes you drive ahead desperately keeping your courage up and covering your shyness by doing something boldly like reading a report aloud in class. But afterward you're a wreck. Putting yourself forward is so costly emotionally that even if you succeed in impressing people you retreat again. Success and recognition hardly seem worth the pain.

Many shy people do manage to compete very effectively. Shy teens have been known to fight like blazes in their own quiet way to be valedictorian of the class. Lots do make it.

There are Olympic gold medalist skaters and famous actors who become physically ill before an exhibition or performance. But they're tough competitors able to do what they must regardless of being shy and terrified about performing and competing.

Shy people are often very sensitive, highly conscious of their own inner reactions. They know when they're frightened, and they have no way of hiding it from themselves. If anything, shy people are often prone to overanalyzing their emotions. But being introspective and reflective may actually help you when you finally get to know people. For one thing, you won't come across as arrogant, pushy, and obnoxious. Shyness can seem very classy. Friends will want to talk to you just because you appear to be a good listener.

Tom and Linda and Bill and Ann

Tom was a shy boy. Linda was a shy girl. Tom was too deep within his own shell to make out with girls. Linda was too withdrawn even to smile at a boy. Nobody knows why some people are shy. Tom had been labeled the quiet kid in the family, and he just seemed to fall in with living up to this particular expectation. Linda's teachers had always considered her shy, and that had proved useful. Linda was never any trouble in school, and teachers confused what was really passivity with attentiveness. She always got "A's" in deportment. Tom was afraid that others would dislike him and hurt him if he revealed "the real me." Linda's whole family was shy, and there are experts who claim that shyness has a genetic basis.

Ann was attractive, popular, and outgoing. So was Bill. But they weren't interested in each other. They were too much alike and would have had a destructively competitive relationship. Ann liked Tom. She considered him sensitive, sincere, and refreshingly nonmacho. Bill liked Linda. He felt he could trust her, rely on her. He sensed that she wouldn't go out with him just to show off and that she wouldn't drop him as soon as someone new came along. His ex-girlfriend, who was very popular, had treated him pretty badly, but then she always had at least two or three boys hanging around waiting to go out with her.

Ann and Bill had to do all the work in the beginning. Ann approached Tom slowly but steadily, first talking to him, then walking down the hall with him. Eventually Tom and Ann had deep serious conversations. Then they kidded around. After that it was prom time. They wound up one of the happiest best-matched couples in the school. Bill got Linda to help him with his homework. Then he got her to say yes to going to see a movie. Soon he was pouring out his most personal thoughts, telling her things he'd never told anyone else. Bill wound up giving Linda his varsity jacket and his senior class ring.

At least shyness is a clear obstacle to very public kinds of competition, yet there are kids who appear to exude confidence and who seem highly competitive but who are really the opposite. When it comes to the crunch, they choke.

Paul

Paul was good-looking, and he never lacked for girlfriends. He was a talented singer, played the trombone, and was a spectacular bicycle racer. Or was he? If Paul had any striking talent, it was the ability to tell convincing lies. True, Paul had lots of girlfriends, but they chose him. He never went out with them long, and the relationship consisted mainly of getting drunk and having sex in the back of his car. He was only comfortable with girls he didn't really like.

When Paul met a girl he really liked, he was incapable of asking her out. Take Mandy. Mandy was intelligent, pretty, and had a strong personality. Paul sat next to her in study hall, and though she flirted with him, he never got up the courage to do more than comb his hair and brag about his numerous conquests. When Mandy got tired of waiting for him and started going out with someone else, Paul was devastated. He pretended publicly that he'd never really cared about Mandy. She was just another girl and he didn't need her.

When it came to singing, Paul refused to join chorus, be in the high school musical, or take voice lessons. He liked to tell people that he was so marvelous he didn't need improvement. So he spent a lot of time at home singing to his mirror alone and dreaming about making it big as a rock star. He also dreamed about winning important bicycle races. Though he practiced steadily, when it came time to enter races he usually backed off. He always had an excuse, a reason, for not carrying plans through. In the end most of his great competitive successes were more talk than reality.

Then there are those who turn noncompeting into an art form. They pretend they are above or outside the rat race but they are actually highly competitive.

George

George was considered an eccentric at his small high school. Possibly the brightest kid in his class, he got high marks easily. With a modest effort he could have been first in his class, but he insisted it wasn't worth the bother. Still, he wasn't a confirmed rebel, the type who won't do any work no matter how intelligent he is. He wasn't a bold risk taker. You'd never catch him getting into serious trouble at school. Unlike his brother who was picked up by the cops for riding his motorcycle while drunk, George was careful. He never got into fights either. He was the school character, not the school criminal.

George refused to participate in any extracurricular activities, even though he read widely and would have been a good editor for the school newspaper. He spoke up aggressively in class, arguing with teachers, insulting other students in a jocular way, and deliberately turning in papers slightly late. In his junior year he announced dramatically that he wasn't going to college, and in his senior year he spurned all scholarship offers. When chastised for lacking ambition, George's comeback was that he might relent and become a chiropractor or an undertaker. Though he really liked Jill, one of the smartest girls in his class, he never asked her out. He never went to dances or parties and, though he had many acquaintances, had no close friends. Last heard from, he was contemplating leaving for Mongolia the day after he graduated from high school.

George had found his own highly individualistic way of expressing competitive spirit and by setting up his own rules and playing games of his own creation he could win all the time at least superficially. Of course, George's obstinancy, though it brought him attention, was potentially very destructive. He was so afraid of what he considered the humiliation of losing that he dared never reveal real feelings or go for anything openly.

Sadly, George is an example of somebody with real gifts in danger of being unable to use his or her talent at all because in the end nobody can compete constantly on his or her own terms. Like it or not we must compete in situations where other people set the guidelines. Learning to face this is one of the basic ingredients in being able to handle competition well.

•11•
HOW TO COMPETE AND SURVIVE

As we have seen, competition is part of everybody's life, yours and ours, in a thousand different ways. Sometimes the competition is clear, other times so subtle we are barely aware of it—but it's still there.

There are no surefire, all-purpose rules for dealing with the many forms of competition. The areas for competition are too varied, the individual responses too complicated. What works for one person in one situation, may be absolutely wrong for another situation or another individual. But still, there are a few steps anyone can take to compete more successfully and more happily.

Basically these steps are all common sense, but common sense, as we all know, is sometimes not so common. So the rules are worth repeating.

1. WHAT AM I DOING? AND WHY AM I DOING IT?

It's often a good idea to step back for a moment and ask yourself some simple questions like "What am I doing?" and "Why am I doing it?"

134

Let's say that you have decided to run for class president. What you're doing seems fairly obvious; you're running for school office. But it's not really that simple. You know, everybody knows, that the class president has no real power. Despite a speech in which you make vague promises about doing things for your class, you know you probably won't do any more or any less than others who are running. All the really important decisions are made by the faculty and the administration.

School elections are a popularity contest—they are not a measure of how popular your policies are; they are a measure of how popular *you* are. So what you're really doing is taking part in a popularity contest.

Why are you doing it? Well, maybe you want to prove to yourself that you're well liked or perhaps prove to others that you are. Maybe you want to spoil the chances of some other kid who has been your enemy since elementary school. Maybe you figure that the title Class President will look good on your college application. None of these motives has anything to do with actually being class president, but they are all very human motives, and we wouldn't criticize you or anyone for having them. Even revenge, though it is rarely as satisfying as one thinks it will be, is a perfectly ordinary human motive.

But be quite clear in your own mind before you become involved in any competitive situation that can be exhausting and painful what you are really doing and why you are doing it and what you really hope to win. That leads us right to point number 2.

2. KNOW YOURSELF.

That may be the oldest piece of advice in the world. It's what Socrates used to tell his students. It's advice that's easy to give and hard to carry out. But it is certainly worth trying.

Let's go back to the example of that school election. Before you actually get engaged in that kind of competition, you will have to assess your own strengths and weaknesses. Can you actually get up and make a speech without making a fool of yourself or feeling like one? Can you go around greeting people you don't know, or don't know very well, or even people you don't like very much and ask for their vote? Do you honestly believe that you have enough friends in your class to stand a chance at winning? Do you really care about winning? Will you be crushed if you lose? Are you prepared to spend the time and energy doing whatever is required to do a good job in the office if you do win? Both losing and winning have a price attached. Before you jump in, be sure you are prepared to pay the price.

3. BE YOURSELF.

This follows logically from knowing yourself.

Let's return to our hypothetical class election and assume that, after weighing all the alternatives and asking all the questions, you've decided to run anyway. Let's further assume that you're a rather prickly character. You make loyal friends, but you make enemies as well. Nothing wrong with that; lots of us are prickly characters. But you can't suddenly change from what you are into Miss Sweetiepie or Harry Handshake. No one is going to believe that transformation, and if you try, you will doubtless feel like an idiot.

Obviously you shouldn't go out of your way to antagonize potential supporters, unless of course you don't really want to win. Be as friendly as you can. Emphasize your strong points. But don't try to become someone else.

Unless you are a great actor, it won't work. That sort of pretense is also degrading. If being untrue to yourself is what it takes to win, then the prize isn't worth it.

4. GIVE IT YOUR BEST SHOT.

Once you've decided actually to go after a particular goal that is important to you, then you owe it to yourself to try your best.

Sometimes people don't try very hard because they're not all that interested. Or they've changed their mind and decided it isn't worth the effort. That's fair enough. You can't knock yourself out over everything.

There are, however, others who don't try because they are already defeated. They're sure they can't win anyway, so they ask, "Why bother?" And there are those who don't try very hard so that they have a built-in excuse in case they do fail. "Well I would have won if I had really tried."

Neither of these reasons, particularly the second, is adequate or helpful. We're not going to claim that if you adopt a "winning attitude" you inevitably will win. That's nonsense. Winning depends on a huge number of factors, including luck, over which you have absolutely no control. But what you do have control over is your own performance, be it on a test, on stage, on the athletic field, or on a date. Win or lose, you should be able to look back and say, "Well, I did the best I could." And you should be able to mean it. Getting in the habit of doing your best, even when you don't win, will be very useful.

5. SET REASONABLE GOALS.

Psychologists and therapists who deal with the problems created by competition always urge their clients and patients to set reasonable goals for themselves—it's excellent advice. But you're young, so that advice has to be amended a bit. Reasonable goals are more important when you're thirty than when you're sixteen. Hang on to your long-term goals, even your dreams. Don't start scaling down your ambitions until you have really tried. Don't be afraid to try for more than you might reasonably achieve. If you want to try out for the team or run for office, go for it, even if your chances of making the team or winning the election are small. Apply to that dream college that takes only 10 percent of its applicants. Don't be afraid to try. The penalty for failure is not death or disgrace.

In the short term, however, reasonable and achievable goals are vital. If you want to get along better with your brother, don't think in terms of an instant transformation. Go a step at a time. The next time he irritates you, try not fighting with him. It can become a habit for both of you, and that may ultimately change your relationship.

If you can't make it as a cheerleader, you might be able to join the school chorus. That doesn't have the same status, but it's a whole lot better than sitting around and sulking and feeling that nobody loves you.

6. DON'T KEEP BANGING YOUR HEAD AGAINST THE WALL.

There is an old saying, "If at first you don't succeed, try, try again." That's fine, as far as it goes, but sometimes it goes too far. Maybe you've run in those class elections for three years now, and you've lost every time. You've given it your best shot, but you seem to be losing ground, and you feel absolutely miserable after every loss. You're beginning to think that you have no friends at all. But you say to yourself, "I'm no quitter. I'll show them. I'll run again!"

Actually the time may have come to give up on the

elections and turn your attention elsewhere. Pursuing that particular goal is becoming destructive. No one can lose all the time and remain unaffected. The confidence of even the most secure will be shaken by repeated defeats. If you've given it your best shot, there is no shame in giving up. You're not a quitter. You're not weak. Sometimes not trying again is just a sign of good sense.

Compete! Go for it! Do it as energetically, indeed as fiercely as you can. Try to be the best. But pick your areas of competition. Throw yourself into competition in things you enjoy or things you feel are really worth while. If you can do that, then win or lose, you're a winner.

BIBLIOGRAPHY

Carnegie, Dale. *How to Win Friends and Influence People*. New York: Pocket Books, 1977.

Cohen, Susan and Daniel. *Teenage Stress*. New York: M. Evans, 1984.

Divine, James, and Kylen, David. *How to Beat Test Anxiety & Score Higher on the SAT & All Other Exams*. Woodbury, NY: Barrons, 1982.

Dobson, James. *Preparing for Adolescence*. New York: Bantam, 1980.

Dyer, Wayne W. *The Sky's the Limit*. New York: Simon and Schuster, 1980.

Freudenberger, Herbert, and Richelson, Geraldine. *Burnout: The High Cost of Achievement*. New York: Doubleday, 1980.

Gardner, John W. *Excellence: Can We Be Equal and Excellent Too*. New York: Harper & Row, 1961.

Hill, Napoleon. *Think and Grow Rich*. New York: Hawthorne Books, 1966.

James, Muriel, and Jongeward, Dorothy. *Born to Win*. Reading, MA: Addison-Wesley, 1971.

Kassorla, Irene. *Go for It!* New York: Delacorte Press, 1984.

McCoy, Kathleen. *Coping with Teenage Depression*. New American Library, New York: 1982.

Norman, Jane, and Harris, Myron. *The Private Life of the American Teenager*. New York: Rawson & Wade, 1981.

Bibliography

Owen, David. *None of the Above*. Boston: Houghton Mifflin, 1985.

Reit, Seymor V. *Sibling Rivalry*. New York: Ballantine Books, 1985.

Rose, Margaret Ann. *Rush—A Girl's Guide to Sorority Success*. New York: Villard Books, 1985.

Ringer, Robert J. *Looking Out for Number One*. New York: Funk & Wagnals, 1977.

——————. *Winning Through Intimidation*. Beverly Hills, CA: Los Angeles Book Publishers, 1974.

Ruben, Harvey L. *Competing*. New York: Harper & Row, 1980.

Sharpe, Robert, and Lewis, David. *The Success Factor*. New York: Crown, 1977.

Tech, Leon. *The Fear of Success*. New York: NAL, 1978.

Waitley, Dennis. *The Winner's Edge*. New York: Times Books, 1980.

Weston, Carol. *Girltalk*. New York: Barnes & Noble, 1985.

Westheimer, Ruth, and Kravatz, Nathan. *First Love*. New York: Warner Books, 1975.

Zimbardo, Philip G. *Shyness. What It Is. What to Do About It*. Reading, MA: Addison-Wesley, 1977.